5-Step
TOEFL Prep
for Hindi Speakers

GREG BRITT

All inquires should be addressed to:
BSL Books, under the direction of
Britt Servicios Lingûísticos
Insurgentes Sur 56-4, Colonia Juárez,
06600 México D.F., México
Tel., 52 5207 9516, email: info@dfbritt.com
www.dfbritt.com

TOEFL is a registered trademark of Educational Testing Service. This publication is NOT endorsed nor approved by ETS. BSL Books bears sole responsibility
for this book's content and is not connected with ETS.

ISBN: 1492765465
ISBN-13: 978-1492765462

Some material in this book was adapted from
TOEFL Prep for Spanish Speakers,
by Greg Britt.

Hindi translations by Bharat Dewan
Design and editing by Asad Larik

5-Step
TOEFL Prep
for Hindi Speakers

Table of Contents

TOEFL Prep

for Hindi Speakers

QUICK CHECK
Grammar Problem Areas

STEP ONE

> MC	Main Clause
SC	Subordinate Clause

STEP TWO

S=V	Subject-Verb Agreement
S=P	Subject-Pronoun Agreement
VTF	Verb Tense or Form
PFR	Pronoun Form or Reference

STEP THREE

VBL	Verbals
WF	Word Form

STEP FOUR

WO	Word Order
PS	Parallel Structure
UR	Unnecessary Repetition

STEP FIVE

CU	Correct Usage

Main Clauses

Structures that Function as Subjects

Gerunds vs. Verbs

Repeated Subjects & Omitted Verbs

EXERCISE SWE-1

Directions: Using the abbreviations that identify each type of error, classify the following twelve (one of each type) errors, then try to correct the errors. In future exercises like this one, try to cover the answers and practice classifying the errors based on the twelve we've reviewed.

MC   1.   A subject it must not be repeated within a clause.

VBL   2.   *To Kill a Mockingbird,* which was written by Harper Lee, is a very interested book.

WO   3.   The child was just barely enough tall to reach the sink.

PS   4.   Among his many hobbies, he enjoys to cook, swimming, and reading.

UR   5.   Although he worked many hours on his document, the final draft was concise and succinct.

SC   6.   The new restaurant is quiet popular, although is very expensive.

S=V   7.   The swimming instructor, along with his 30 students, are swimming the breast stroke.

WF   8.   The usage of drugs among teenagers is sometimes a result of an emotion problem.

Remember that in English adjectives always come before the word *enough.*

CU   9. Diet sodas have less calories than normal ones.

VTF   10. The little boy could not reach the coins that had fell behind the sofa.

S=P   11. Everybody in the class will give their oral report today.

PFR   12. The lifeguard doesn't allow us running around the pool.

NOTE: The ⊙ symbol, as found before question number 3 of this exercise, should be given special attention. When you see this symbol, always check the bottom of the page for an important explanation of a grammatical or idiomatic element (or a vocabulary word) that might cause problems.

By definition, every complex sentence contains a *main clause* and at least one *subordinate clause.* Both the main clauses and subordinate clauses have a subject and a verb, but only the main clause can function independently as a sentence. The subordinate clause depends upon the main clause and cannot function alone. It is possible to have a main clause with no subordination, but you cannot correctly have a subordinate clause without first having a main clause to support it.

We will begin with a study of main clauses. When you have a **MC** error it will usually involve a repeated subject or an omitted verb. In rare occasions, you might find a repeated verb or a missing subject. In order to help identify such errors with the subject and verb of the main clause, we will review the five types of structures that function as subjects in English, followed by a review of verb identification.

एक वाक्य , ((a sentence) प्रधान (मुख्य) अथवा गौण
उपवाक्य, में एक विषय तथा एक क्रिया अवश्य होनी चाहिए ।
दोनों में से किसी एक को भी छोड़ा नहीं जा सकता ।

There are five structures that can function as **subjects** in English. They are: the noun, pronoun, gerund, infinitive, and noun clause. Let's look at an example of each.

1.	**Noun**	The <u>teacher</u> is very nice.
2.	**Pronoun**	<u>He</u> is very nice.
3.	**Gerund**	<u>Learning</u> is fun.
4.	**Infinitive**	<u>To learn</u> is fun.
5.	**Noun Clause**	<u>That we attend class</u> is important.

Notice that the pronoun is used to replace a simple noun subject. Also notice that the gerund and infinitive are interchangeable as subjects.

Try not to confuse gerunds for verbs. Remember: *A gerund is a gerund, a verb is a verb. A gerund is never a verb.* The problem is that we often conveniently call everything with "ing" a *gerund*. That is not the case. By definition, a gerund is not a verb and must have some form of the verb *to be* before to "activate" it as a verb. Compare the following: **Gerunds:** swimming, playing, reading. **Verbs:** is swimming, were playing, have been reading. Also keep in mind that an infinitive needs to be joined with a conjugated verb to function as a verb.

Perhaps the most difficult of the five subject structures is the noun clause. The noun clause is a type of subordinate clause and has its own subject and verb. If you are confused, go to the verb and ask yourself, "what?" *What is important?* **That we attend class.** The answer will lead you to the noun clause. In fact, anytime you have trouble locating your subject, always go to the verb which should lead you to the source of its action—the subject.

EXERCISE SWE-2

Directions: Find and underline the subject in the main clause in each sentence. Then classify it, putting the number of the corresponding subject form in the blank.
1. Noun, 2. Pronoun, 3. Gerund, 4. Infinitive, 5. Noun Clause

   2   1. <u>She</u> will attend college at an American university.

_____ 2. Fishing is a popular sport in Miami.

_____ 3. This is my sister's book.

_____ 4. Breathing contaminated air causes respiratory problems.

_____ 5. Whoever finds the lost puppy will be rewarded.

_____ 6. Tornadoes arise when conditions that cause ordinary thunderstorms are unusually violent.

_____ 7. To drive a bus requires special training.

_____ 8. Mumps is a contagious disease in which the salivary glands swell.

_____ 9. Papyrus is a reed-like plant belonging to the family of sedges.

_____ 10. Falling down stairs might result in serious injury.

_____ 11. That pigeons can find their way home is an amazing ability.

_____ 12. Subjects should not be repeated within a clause.

_____ 13. To study for long periods of time is not recommended.

_____ 14. Silk is the thread or cloth made from the fine web of the silkworm.

_____ 15. Advertising is considered a science as well as an art.

Now we will practice identifying the verb(s) of main and subordinate clauses.

EXERCISE SWE-3

Directions: Find all the verbs and all parts of each verb in the main and subordinate clauses. Draw a line under each part, as in the example.

1. The second largest public square is located in the historical district of Mexico City.

2. The lilies will begin blooming around Easter.

3. There should have been more discussion before a decision was reached.

4. Unlimited information is available on the Internet.

5. Several months are sometimes necessary to adequately prepare for the TOEFL exam.

6. Spanish is not widely spoken in Brazil.

7. The doctor was sued on malpractice charges due to gross negligence.

8. Although it was the world's most popular language, Latin is now considered rather unimportant.

9. Housework, including washing dishes, vacuuming rugs, and cleaning floors, is no longer done exclusively by women.

10. There will be a short delay before the start of the movie.

11.   The country's political system has seen sweeping changes in recent history.

12.   The introduction of longer tennis rackets has given players more powerful serves.

13.   Citizens of the United States are discouraged from travelling to Cuba.

14.   David Letterman is considered by many to be the funniest talk show host on TV.

15.   Many scholarships are available to international students who score above 550 on the TOEFL.

Before we continue our study of **MC** errors, we'll take a short break to do a **MINI TOEFL** practice exercise. These exercises are designed exactly like Parts A and B of the actual TOEFL. They are also timed to help simulate the actual exam.

MINI TOEFL-1

Directions: In questions 1-5, choose the one word or phrase that best completes the sentence. In questions 6-10, identify the underlined word(s) that should be changed to make the sentence correct. **TIME: 6 minutes**

1.   Shivering is automatically activated by the temperature of the blood dropping too_____ .

   (A) high   (B) lately
   (C) low   (D) soon

2.   The color of a human being's skin _____ on three pigments which are found in the body.

   (A) designed to be   (B) depends
   (C) belonging   (D) arrives

3.   _____ 1,040 species of amphibians have been identified.

   (A) As many as   (B) As many
   (C) As much as   (D) Much as

4.   A twelve-year-old is not _____ to buy alcoholic beverages.

   (A) as old enough   (B) old enough
   (C) enough old   (D) old as

5.   Researchers are studying many drugs to discover if
_____ cancer.

(A) can they cure   (B) it can cure
(C) they can cure   (D) curing

6.   The congressman <u>which</u> introduced the <u>bill</u> has
                       A   B
been <u>criticized</u> for his <u>questionable</u> judgment.
           C   D

7.   <u>Among</u> the <u>many</u> activities at the kindergarten, the
    A   B
children <u>most enjoy</u> painting, singing, and <u>to play</u>
             C   D
games.

8.   <u>Because</u> Chop Suey <u>is served</u> in nearly all Chinese
     A   B
restaurants, <u>it</u> is not Chinese <u>at all</u>.
         C   D

9.   Not until <u>around</u> 1900 <u>watches did</u> appear on bands
         A   B
to be <u>worn</u> around <u>the</u> wrist.
     C   D

10.   The butterfly <u>has</u> <u>a long, lengthy</u> tube, <u>called</u> a probos-
        A   B   C
cis, through which it can suck the <u>nectar</u> from flowers.
                              D

Remember that **MC** errors normally involve repeated subjects or missing verbs. We've practiced identifying subjects and verbs, and that brings us to a special problem. Many words in English function in many ways—they can function as a verb and another part of speech. If you don't know, for example, that *book* can function as a verb, it could cause problems.

Suppose you're analyzing a sentence—trying to find the subject and verb. You might come across a word like *book* and not recognize it as a verb. After concluding that the sentence has no verb it is easy to begin "inventing" errors that don't really exist.

The following exercise will help you recognize many problematic words that typically function as verbs or as other parts of speech. It is important that you understand their verbal and non-verbal meanings.

EXERCISE SWE-4

Directions: Many of the following words can function in different ways. In the blank, write **AV** if the word *always* functions as a verb, **NV** if it *never* functions as a verb, and **B** if it can function *both* as a verb and another part of speech. Consider the word only as it is written with no changes.

1.	_B_	sleep	11.	____	clean
2.	____	need	12.	____	paint
3.	____	window	13.	____	close
4.	____	might	14.	____	hope
5.	____	open	15.	____	can
6.	____	trip	16.	____	cure
7.	____	observe	17.	____	house
8.	____	warm	18.	____	will
9.	____	advice	19.	____	elevate
10.	____	laugh	20.	____	smoke

Can you think of other words that can function as verbs and other parts of speech? If you're studying alone, try to make a short list. If you're working with a group, try playing a word game—take turns naming a "tricky" word.

Three words can function as auxiliary verbs and should be given special attention. They are: *might, can,* and *will.* Let's take a closer look at their functions.

QUICK CHECK

	AUXILIARY VERB	**NOUN**
MIGHT	EXPRESSES POSSIBILITY I might go to the beach this week-end.	power, strength
CAN	EXPRESSES ABILITY I can speak English.	container for food or garbage
WILL	EXPRESSES FUTURE I will take the TOEFL soon.	the legal document

Again, make sure you understand the verbal and non-verbal meanings of all of the above "tricky" words (as well as any you might have added). We'll continue in the next exercise reviewing "tricky" words—words that can function as a verb and another part of speech. Pay attention to the function of the word in each particular sentence—watch out for new words that are not included in the previous exercise.

EXERCISE SWE-5

Directions: Carefully read the following sentences. Based on the sentence structure, if the underlined word is a verb, write **V** in the blank. If it functions as another part of speech, write **X** in the blank.

<u>X</u>   1. After Alice received the telegram, all <u>hope</u> of resolving the difficult situation disappeared.

_____ 2. Experienced travelers who desire nothing more than to relax and read <u>book</u> travel on Amtrak trains.

_____ 3. It seems every Easter Sunday is beautiful and sunny and the kids always <u>spring</u> from their beds at the crack of dawn to find their Easter baskets full of goodies.

_____ 4. With my left eye closed, I can view <u>close</u> images with my right eye.

_____ 5. The executives met for several hours in the meeting room and finally decided to <u>table</u> the motion.

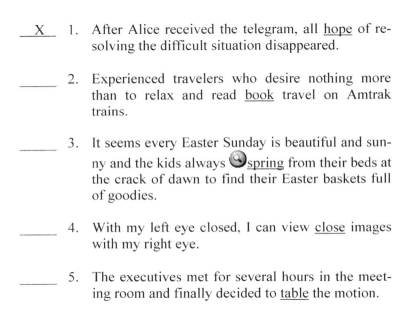

"spring": के चार अर्थ है : 1. एक मौसम , 2. छलांग लगाना 3. पानी का प्राकृतिक स्रोत 4. कुंडलित तार (like in a watch).

_____ 6. Although Mike remained in bed for hours, he wasn't able to get much <u>sleep</u>.

_____ 7. With the idea of lots of money dancing around in his head, he was able to <u>bank</u> a shot and win the pool tournament.

_____ 8. Due to carelessness, one <u>can</u> fell on the floor.

_____ 9. While in the airport newsstand reading a book, Johar heard the <u>page</u> and ran for the departing flight.

_____ 10. Tomorrow morning the <u>will</u> of the deceased is scheduled to be reviewed by the family attorney.

_____ 11. The small raft suddenly hit a reef and began to <u>rock</u>.

_____ 12. Wearing his new suit, Tom misspelled the last word and had to settle for a <u>tie</u>.

_____ 13. With tears of desperation rolling down her cheeks, the woman sent out a shrill <u>cry</u> for help.

_____ 14. Don't <u>trip</u> on the wet deck of the boat.

Compare *one can fell on the floor* and *one can fall on the floor.* We can often tell if what is sometimes an auxiliary verb is functioning as a verb or noun by examining the verb that follows—if that verb is conjugated, it is functioning as a noun. If it is not, it is functioning as an auxiliary verb

_____ 15. Like many animals, the raccoon <u>mothers</u> its babies until they can survive on their own.

_____ 16. The convention hotel can <u>house</u> all of the members of the association, but you're welcome to stay in our home.

_____ 17. Check your watches so that we can <u>time</u> this exercise.

_____ 18. Even if they never become reality, <u>dreams</u> are an important source of inspiration.

_____ 19. In Edgar Allen Poe's "The Raven", there is frequent reference to a <u>knocking</u> at his chamber door.

_____ 20. While Ginger was gathering flowers from the garden, the sun <u>rose</u>.

Before we begin our study of **SC** (Subordinate Clause) errors, it will be useful to review the difference between clauses and phrases. A clause has a subject and verb, but a phrase is simply a group of words without a subject and active verb.

The following exercise will give you practice distinguishing between **clauses** and **phrases**. In order to do this you will need to pay attention to gerund and infinitive subjects—try not to confuse them for verbs. Remember a gerund does not function as a verb without being connected with some form of the verb *to be* and an infinitive needs to be connected with a conjugated verb to function as an active verb.

EXERCISE SWE-6

Directions: Examine the function of each word in the following sentences to determine if it is a **clause** or a **phrase**. In the blank, put **C** for clauses and **P** for phrases.

_C_ 1. waiting is annoying

_____ 2. the child walking down the street

_____ 3. to study Japanese every day

_____ 4. money makes the world go 'round

_____ 5. seeing is believing

_____ 6. reservations are necessary

_____ 7. predicting the weather is tricky

_____ 8. smoking is not always socially acceptable

_____ 9. pronouncing the alphabet

_____ 10. waiting a long time for the bus

_____ 11. winning is not everything

_____ 12. baking chocolate chip cookies

_____ 13. arriving after the closing of the shop

_____ 14. painting is a form of artistic expression

_____ 15. dams generate electricity

Remember, **MC** errors normally have a repeated subject or missing verb in the main clause. In rare instances you might find a repeated verb or missing subject. You should now be able to easily identify subjects and verbs (while avoiding confusion with words that function in different ways), gerunds, and infinitives. An important point to keep in mind: repeated subjects are the easiest errors to identify on the TOEFL exam.

EXERCISE SWE-7

Directions: The following sentences are supposed to be correct main clauses. Some of them are correct, but some of them repeat the subject or do not have a verb. In the blank write **OK** if the sentence is correct, **minus (-)** if the verb is missing, and **plus (+)** if the subject is repeated.

___+___ 1. The world's first subway it opened in London.

_____ 2. The bears dancing in the circus.

_____ 3. Ivory comes from the tusks of elephants.

_____ 4. Penicillin it is one of the most important medical discoveries of our time.

_____ 5. All of the students with their teacher.

_____ 6. Exercising is good for the heart.

_____ 7. The lioness with its three cubs.

_____ 8. Forms of reading and writing in nearly all civilizations.

_____ 9. Capital punishment it is very controversial in the U.S.

_____ 10. The amount of blood in a person's body depends on his size.

_____ 11. The bus full of passengers crashed.

_____ 12. The test taken by the students.

_____ 13. The Pope he heads Vatican City.

_____ 14. No two fingerprints exactly alike.

_____ 15. The little girl practicing the violin.

In the **MINI TOEFL** that follows, try to find **MC** errors—usually repeated subjects or missing verbs. However, all of the errors in this practice exercise and those that follow will not be directly related to the specific point you're studying. There will be a few unrelated errors. This is because it is important to recognize errors, but also important to recognize correct structures. If you know in advance that all of the errors are related to a specific point, you might not get the practice you need recognizing correct structures.

MINI TOEFL-2

Directions: In questions 1-5, choose the one word or phrase that best completes the sentence. In questions 6-10, identify the underlined word(s) that should be changed to correct the sentence. **TIME: 6 minutes.**

1.   The unicorn _____ a mythical animal that never actually existed.

     (A) it was   (B) was
     (C) believed   (D) only

2.   Asparagus _____ a member of the lily family and has many varieties.

     (A) belonging to   (B) it is
     (C) is   (D) grows

3.   Erosion _____ the action whereby land is slowly diminished by water.

     (A) it is   (B) is that
     (C) being   (D) is

4.   _____ that the world's first postage stamp appeared in England.

     (A) It was in 1847   (B) Because in 1847
     (C) That is 1847   (D) In 1847 that it was

5.   The hamburger _____ name from its place of origin, Hamburg, Germany.

       (A) and its   (B) got its
       (C) along with its   (D) it got its

6.   Atlanta, home of the 1996 Olympic Games, <u>it</u> is the
                                                  A
       <u>capital</u> of Georgia and <u>the</u> largest city in the <u>southern</u>
            B   C   D
       U.S.

7.   The Boeing 747, <u>which was</u> first flown in 1969, <u>it is</u>
                          A   B
       the <u>biggest</u> jetliner <u>in</u> the world.
            C   D

8.   Although Delaware <u>the second</u> smallest state <u>in the</u>
                            A   B
       Union, <u>it is</u> the <u>first state</u> of the U.S.
                C   D

9.   Based on <u>population,</u> Tokyo <u>it is</u> the <u>largest</u> city
                   A   B   C
       <u>in the</u> world.
        D

10.   <u>The</u> Great Wall of China, <u>constructed completely</u> by
        A   B
       hand, <u>it runs a length</u> of 1,500 miles.
              C   D

5-Step
TOEFL Prep
for Hindi Speakers

QUICK CHECK
Grammar Problem Areas

STEP ONE

MC	Main Clause
> SC	Subordinate Clause

STEP TWO

S=V	Subject-Verb Agreement
S=P	Subject-Pronoun Agreement
VTF	Verb Tense or Form
PFR	Pronoun Form or Reference

STEP THREE

VBL	Verbals
WF	Word Form

STEP FOUR

WO	Word Order
PS	Parallel Structure
UR	Unnecessary Repetition

STEP FIVE

CU	Correct Usage

Subordination

Noun Clauses

Adjective Clauses

Adverb Clauses

EXERCISE SWE-8

Directions: Using the abbreviations that identify each type of error, cover the answers and classify the following ten errors, then try to correct the errors. Only ten of the twelve types of errors are listed in order to minimize "elimination" guessing.

PFR   1. The young man who Claudia wants to marry lives in California.

WO   2. It would be an understatement to say that Cinderella met interesting someone at the gala event.

VBL   3. After buying groceries at the market, dinner was prepared.

PS   4. This year our football team is expected to be strong, talented, and know that it takes hard work to win.

UR   5. Aside from the fact that Carol is opposed to the use of real animal fur, she found the coat far too expensive and costly.

WF   6. Styles may come and go, but traditionally tailoring like cuffed pants and button down shirts will always be in fashion for men.

MC   7. Although he had always been a clown, Bozo he wanted to learn the flying trapeze.

S=P   8. Everyone in the class hopes to achieve a high score on their TOEFL exam.

S=V   9.   Neither the director nor the choir members likes the lyrics.

SC   10. Alcohol is actually a narcotic stimulates the brain.

By definition, every 🔍**complex sentence** contains at least two elements: a **main clause** and at least one **subordinate clause**. It might contain several subordinate clauses and phrases, but as a minimum it must contain a main clause and a subordinate clause. Can you remember the main difference and similarity between a main and subordinate clause?

🔍
एक मिश्रित वाक्य में कम से कम दो उपवाक्य होने चाहिए , प्रधान उपवाक्य तथा गौण उपवाक्य । प्रधान उपवाक्य में विषय और क्रिया होते हैं जो एक संपूर्ण वाक्य बनाते हैं । गौण उपवाक्य में विषय और क्रिया होते हैं परन्तु ये एक स्वतंत्र रूप में वाक्य नहीं बनाते हैं , ये अर्थ के लिए प्रधान उपवाक्य पर निर्भर होते हैं । एक गौण उपवाक्य विशेषण , क्रिया विशेषण अथवा क्रिया की तरह भी काम कर सकता है । एक वाक्य शब्दों का एक समूह होता है जिसमे सक्रिय क्रिया नहीं होती । एक वाक्य में गौण उपवाक्य अथवा वाक्यांश तभी हो सकते हैं जब उसमे एक प्रधान उपवाक्य हो ।

QUICK CHECK

SUBORDINATE CLAUSE	DESCRIPTION	EXAMPLE
NOUN	Functions as subject or object of main clause	*What the teacher said* surprised the class.
ADJECTIVE	Always follows and describes a noun	The book *which I am reading* is interesting.
ADVERB	Always begins with an adverbial conjunction	*Although it is very dangerous,* many people like hang gliding.

As we begin our study of **SC** errors keep in mind that **focusing on the main clause will help you identify the subordinate clause**. It's also useful to identify **phrases** so that they can be "thrown away". Phrases (with the exception of verbal phrases, which we will study in the VBL section) rarely play an important grammatical role in the sentence and usually have nothing to do with the error. They only cause confusion. Again, focus your attention on identifying the main and subordinate clauses, while eliminating phrases from consideration.

Subordination is vitally important to your success on the TOEFL. We must learn to quickly analyze sentences to find errors. A good understanding of subordination will provide you with the foundation you need to analyze many other types of errors. You will see that many of the problem areas that we will study require that we first separate our sentence, finding the main and subordinate clauses. For example, we can't really know if we have a repeated subject if we don't first know which subject goes with which clause. What at first might seem like an error may actually be correct because every clause must have a subject.

We will study three types if subordinate clauses: the **noun, adjective,** and **adverb** clauses.

Noun clauses, as we saw in the **MC** point, can function as subjects (along with nouns, pronouns, gerunds, and infinitives). They can also function as objects of main clauses. The noun clause is perhaps the most difficult of all clauses to understand because it cannot be completely separated from the main clause (the adjective and adverb clauses can). The noun clause becomes an integral part of the main clause, functioning as subject or object.

Noun clauses are typically *marked* with introductory words, or subordinating signals, such as: that, why, what, how, or where. We will learn to recognize noun clauses using these words. But do not become too dependent on them because we will also see *unmarked* noun clauses that have no introductory words. Try to focus more on the sentence structure. Remember the noun clause functions as a noun (in meaning) but has its own subject and verb. It will serve as the subject or object of the main clause.

Let's examine few examples of each:

NOUN CLAUSE SUBJECTS

<u>That Eric arrived two hours late</u> made his mother angry.

<u>What the boy said</u> made his friend sad.

 <u>How he can afford to buy a new car</u> is a mystery to me.

NOUN CLUASE OBJECTS

We didn't hear <u>what the teacher said</u>.

The university catalog explains <u>how students can apply for scholarships</u>.

I know <u>where my pet snake is hiding</u>.

Subordinate **Adjective** clauses are fairly easy to recognize because they *always* follow the noun (or possibly pronoun) that they describe. Obliviously, it would be impossible to begin a sentence with an adjective clause. In fact, adjective clauses are often found in the middle of the main clause. They begin with subordinating signals such as: who, that, which, or when. Again, do not focus entirely on the introductory words—the adjective clause can also be *unmarked*.

 संज्ञा वाक्यांश को पहचानना सबसे कठिन है क्यूंकि प्रधान उपवाक्य में विषय और विधेय की तरह काम करते हुए भी इसका अपना विषय और क्रिया होती है । अगर आप को इस उपवाक्य में कोई कठिनाई है तो ,एक प्रश्न पूछने की कोशिश कीजिए : मेरे लिए एक क्या रहस्य है ? उतर आपको संज्ञा भाग तक ले जाएगा ।

ADJECTICE CLAUSES

Baseball, <u>which is America's favorite pastime</u>, is actually a British invention.

Acupuncture is an ancient Chinese treatment <u>which is still used in many parts of the world</u>.

None of the students know the teacher <u>who is substituting for their English class</u>.

Subordinate **Adverb** clauses are usually found in the beginning or end of a sentence. They *always* begin with subordinating signals (they are never *unmarked*). They begin with what we call *adverbial conjunctions*. These are the words such as: although, as soon as, before, and since.

ADVERB CLAUSES

We decided not to swim in the sea <u>because the water looked dirty</u>.

<u>Although it is very long</u>, *Gone with the Wind* remains a favorite movie.

<u>While they were walking down the beach</u>, the couple enjoyed the sunset.

We will begin our study of **SC** errors by distinguishing between main clauses and subordinate clauses. Remember, they both have a subject and a verb, but the main clause can function independently while the subordinate clause can't. The following exercise will help you distinguish between the two.

EXERCISE SWE-9

Directions: Decide if the following sentences are **main clauses** or **subordinate clauses**. In the blanks, write **MC** for main clauses and **SC** for subordinate clauses.

SC   1. if we are able to arrive two hours before the opening

_____   2. singing is an important element of the church service

_____   3. since we arrived home from our Hawaii vacation

_____   4. hard study is necessary to pass the course

_____   5.   that oranges are a great source of vitamin C

_____   6. "surfing the web" is popular among teenagers

_____   7. even though the U.S. is located south of Canada

_____   8. as soon as the rainy season is over

_____   9. as if the car were newly painted

_____ 10. jumping rope increases the heart rate

_____ 11. the little boy is pretending to be asleep

ध्यान दे अगर आपने वाक्य को "वो संतरे" अथवा "वो संतरा है" में बदला है तो आपके पास एक प्रधान उपवाक्य जरुर होगा ।

_____ 12. when you called me on the phone from Taipei

_____ 13. that we would experience severe flooding

_____ 14. that diamonds are more valuable than gold

_____ 15. if they could see me now

Now we'll distinguish between subordinate clauses and phrases. Remember that a subordinate clause has a subject and verb. A phrase is a group of words that does not contain a subject and an active verb. Again, phrases should usually be "thrown away" when analyzing sentences to find errors. In the following exercise, we will distinguish between subordinate clauses and phrases by checking the sentence for a subject and verb. Be careful with infinitive and gerund subjects—try not to confuse them for verbs.

EXERCISE SWE-10

Directions: Examine the following sentences and write **SC** in the blank for **subordinate clauses.** Mark an (**X**) for **phrases**.

___X___ 1. after returning home from the movie

_____ 2. a self-cleaning oven

_____ 3. because the flight had been cancelled

_____ 4. that he knew the answer to the question

_____ 5. the most sophisticated system available

_____ 6. which he knew nothing about

_____ 7. although he later changed his mind

_____ 8. speaking Korean like a native speaker

_____ 9. to study every day for the TOEFL exam

_____ 10. since he graduated from college

_____ 11. what he did on vacation

_____ 12. to see the animals in the zoo

_____ 13. whom he wants to marry

_____ 14. as soon as tickets go on sale

_____ 15. unless he improves his study habits

Now we'll combine the material studied in the last two exercises and try to distinguish among main clauses, subordinate clauses, and phrases.

EXERCISE SWE-11

Directions: Examine the following sentences and in the blanks write **MC** for **main clauses**, **SC** for **subordinate clauses**, and **(X)** for **phrases**.

__X__ 1. looking at the snow through the small window

_____ 2. his wishes for a better job

_____ 3. 🔍 because of the severe freeze

_____ 4. because the children were beginning to get tired

_____ 5. to play a musical instrument

_____ 6. the tulips bloom in the spring

_____ 7. an elderly couple strolling down the street

_____ 8. in one ear and out the other

_____ 9. the coconut is the fruit of the palm tree

_____ 10. who came to New World with Columbus

_____ 11. about the size of a boulder

🔍 नोट करें *because of* एक वाक्य को परिचित करवाता है ,जबकि *because* एक गौण उपवाक्य को परिचित करवाता है ।

_____ 12. as soon as the clock strikes twelve

_____ 13. pronouncing words in French

_____ 14. to taste fine wines by the glass

_____ 15. after the director's talk is over

When analyzing a TOEFL question, you should first divide your sentence. Find your main clause, subordinate clause(s), and phrase(s). Ask yourself two key questions: 1) *what do I have?* and 2) *what do I need?* First try to find the main clause. If you don't have a main clause, determine what you need to make one. Without exception, **every TOEFL question must have a main clause** (and never more than one).

Sometimes it is necessary to eliminate a word or words to create a main clause. It is typical on the TOEFL to find a sentence that starts with a main clause subject and continues with two or more subordinate clauses. The subject is left "suspended" with no support of a main clause and the subordinate clauses are also left unsupported. *The solution to this type of error is to eliminate a subordinating signal, which will create a main clause.* Examine the following sample question.

Oliver Twist <u>which</u> was written by Charles Dickens
           A

who <u>also wrote</u> <u>numerous other</u> novels before dying <u>on</u>
     B   C   D
June 9, 1870.

In this sentence, the error is A. Notice that if you eliminate the subordinating signal "which" you create a main clause that supports the subject "Charles Dickens" as well as the other subordinate clause and phrase.

If you determine that you have a complete main clause (*what do I have?*) you should next try to complete the sentence *(what do I need?)* with 1) a subordinate clause, 2) a phrase, or 3) a connecting word such as "and" and another verb to extend the main clause.

Before we study the different types of subordinate clauses individually, try to apply these principles of subordination to the TOEFL context. The following TOEFL practice contains several typical subordination **(SC)** errors, as well as some un-related errors.

MINI TOEFL-3

Directions: In questions 1-5, choose the one word or phrase that best completes the sentence. In questions 6-10, identify the underlined word(s) that should be changed to correct the sentence. **TIME: 6 minutes.**

_____ 1. Hong Kong, which has returned to Chinese rule, _____ a British territory.

    (A) that   (B) with
    (C) was   (D) being

_____ 2. Everest, _____ the tallest mountain in the world, is located in the Himalayas.

(A) which is   (B) who is
(C) is   (D) it's

_____ 3. Vincent Van Gogh _____ for his post-impressionist paintings.

(A) who is known   (B) is renowned
(C) being   (D) known

_____ 4. Many people cannot believe _____ has actually walked on the moon.

(A) which he   (B) men
(C) really   (D) that man

_____ 5. When a muscle contracts _____ lactic acid which causes tiredness.

(A) they produce   (B) producing
(C) it produces   (D) causes

_____ 6. The Tower of London <u>which</u> was <u>built by</u> William
                                            A   B
the Conqueror who <u>played</u> an important role in
                                           C
<u>British history</u>.
       D

_____ 7. At the start of a piece of music is found the key
          A   B

        signature tells how many sharps and flats are to be
                C   D

        played.

_____ 8. Elizabeth Taylor, who growing up in the U.S., was
                           A   B

        English by birth.
          C   D

_____ 9. New York City, who is nicknamed the "Big Ap-
                     A   B

        ple", has many skyscrapers.
           C   D

_____ 10. Oprah Winfrey who hosted talk show who
                      A   B   C

        is said to be richest woman in the U.S.
               D

Because subordination is so important when analyzing TOEFL questions, we will give further attention to **three types of subordinate clauses**. Of course, it will never be necessary for you to actually classify subordinate clauses on the TOEFL exam. Careful study of the various types of clauses and sentence structures, however, will give you the knowledge and skills necessary for making a quick analysis of a sentence.

We'll begin with **noun clauses** which can function as the subject or object of the main clause. A marked noun clause will begin with the word *that* or an interrogative such as *what, why,* or *how.*

EXERCISE SWE-12

Directions: Some of the following sentences contain noun clauses (which will function as the subject or object of the main clause and begin with the word *that* or an interrogative). If the sentence contains a noun clause write **NC** in the blank. If the sentence does not contain a noun clause write **(X)** in the blank. Underline the noun clauses.

_NC_ 1. <u>That there is life in outer space</u> has not been proven.

_____ 2. Jimmy gave an oral presentation to the group.

_____ 3. I heard that we won the game.

_____ 4. The book explains how children acquire a second language.

_____ 5. Where we shop for fresh vegetables is right around the corner.

_____ 6. Only children believe that the Tooth Fairy really exists.

_____ 7. That it infrequently rains in the desert does not prevent some specially adapted animals from existing.

_____ 8. The association is made up of only English teachers.

_____ 9. The melted rock inside a volcano is called magma.

_____ 10. How much money the politician spent on his campaign remains a mystery.

_____ 11. That cigarettes cause cancer makes them a serious health threat.

_____ 12. Researchers have discovered that about 95% of the population is right handed.

_____ 13. In 1892 an English scientist named Sir Francis Galton discovered that no two fingerprints are the same.

_____ 14. The instruction booklet explains how the microwave oven is operated.

_____ 15. How twins interact during childhood is the subject of her new book.

_____ 16. It is unfortunate for sports fans that the game had to be cancelled because of bad weather.

_____ 17. That student feels that his project is the best.

_____ 18. Scientists believe that dogs and cats are color blind.

_____ 19. How the brain functions is being studied by medical students.

_____ 20. Delaware is sometimes called "The Diamond State" because of its great value in proportion to its size.

When a noun clause functions as the object of a main clause, it can be **unmarked**, which means the subordinating signal has been eliminated. Compare the following:

marked noun clause: The teacher felt <u>that</u> her students were improving.

unmarked noun clause: The teacher felt her students were improving.

Both sentences are grammatically correct and both have the same meaning. Can you identify the unmarked noun clauses in the following sentences?

EXERCISE SWE-13

Directions: Underline the **unmarked noun clauses** in the following sentences. If you find it helpful, try replacing the omitted *that*.

1.   We all hope <u>the weather report is accurate</u>.

2.   The little boy said he wanted to be a fireman.

3. The policeman said the man had run a red light.

4. It is obvious the congressman will lose the election.

5. The doctor reported the patient was in stable condition.

6. Some believe crystals have healing powers.

7. The journalist reported the new law had been passed.

8. We all hope we will score above 500 on the TOEFL.

9. The school principal said we will have a fire drill today.

10. The diet plan suggests carbohydrates be limited.

We'll work now with **adjective clauses**—remember an adjective clause always follow a noun (or pronoun) and gives us a description of that noun. *Marked* adjective clauses begin with words such as: *that, when, where, which, who,* etc. Remember, adjective clauses often appear in the *middle* of the main clause.

EXERCISE SWE-14

Directions: Identify and underline all of the **adjective clauses** in the following sentences. The clauses in sentences 1-5 are **marked.** In sentences 6-10 they are **unmarked** (no subordinating signal).

1.   The bad smelling odor of skunks is contained in a liquid <u>that the animal produces</u>.

2.   The liquid which the skunk discharges is called musk.

3.   Musk is produced by two glands which are located near the base of the skunk's tail.

4.   Only a small amount of liquid, which can be smelled from half a mile away, is discharged.

5.   The musk, which can also sting the eyes, can be sprayed up to 12 feet.

6.   Insects skunks eat include beetles, crickets, and grasshoppers.

7.   Two kinds of skunks scientists have classified are the striped and hog-nosed.

8.   The size skunks typically reach is 14 to 19 inches.

9.   The bobcat is one of the few enemies the skunk must avoid.

10. Hog-nosed skunks are the only skunks scientists have found in South America.

When subordinate noun and adjective clauses follow words such as *fact, dream, proof, theory, hope,* etc., they can both begin with *that.* Adjective clauses, <u>but not noun clauses,</u> can also begin with *which.* Starting a noun clause with *which* would be considered an error.

It should sound wrong to begin a noun clause with *which.* If you're not sure, try inserting a form of the verb *to be* between the noun and the clause. Compare:

noun clause: the news (is) <u>that the president resigned</u>.

adjective clause: the news <u>that was reported this morning</u>.

It should sound wrong to say "the news **is** that was reported this morning". You can also look at this from a more logical point of view: the noun clause specifically **states** the news (it answers the question "what is the news?"), while the adjective clause only **describes** it.

The following **strategic tip** might save you some confusion on this rather delicate point: if you have determined that your sentence must be completed with *that* or *which* (in the Sentence Completion section) always choose *that.* The TOEFL never offers two correct choices. More analysis could be required if this type of structure is tested in the Error Identification section. Watch for this type of error while you're focusing on **SC** errors in the following TOEFL practice exercise. Remember to find the main clause first—it will help you identify **SC** errors.

MINI TOEFL-4

Directions: In questions 1-5, choose the one word or phrase that best completes the sentence. In questions 6-10, identify the underlined word(s) that should be changed to correct the sentence. **TIME: 6 minutes**

_____ 1. The media publicized the president's decision _____ would seek re-election.

(A) was that he   (B) which he
(C) and it   (D) that he

_____ 2. _____ hopeful that a cure will be found for the disease.

(A) That is   (B) It is
(C) To be   (D) That it is

_____ 3. Houdini once claimed _____ could escape from within any locked container.

(A) which he   (B) that he
(C) always   (D) to

_____ 4. _____ a book that contains definitions of thousands of words.

(A) An dictionary   (B) That a dictionary is
(C) A dictionary is (D) It

_____ 5. The fact that the ozone is disappearing _____ many environmentalists.

(A) disturbs   (B) disturbing to
(C) disturbance of   (D) disturbing

_____ 6. <u>Many</u> people <u>that</u> bullfighting is not a sport <u>at all</u>,
        A   B   C
but torture of an <u>innocent animal</u>.
               D

_____ 7. Financial <u>advisors</u> know <u>that</u> the best investment is
             A   B
for <u>first time</u> stock market <u>investors</u>.
     C   D

_____ 8. <u>Raised</u> in Monroeville, Alabama, Truman Capote
     A
<u>was</u> an author <u>wrote about</u> American life <u>in the</u>
   B   C   D
Deep South.

_____ 9. The event was not really <u>success</u> <u>because</u> the rain
                          A   B
<u>started</u> early <u>in the afternoon</u>.
   C   D

_____ 10. Dr. Morrison's office <u>is located</u> on the <u>second</u>
                         A   B
floor of the <u>administrative</u> building, a three <u>floors</u>
             C   D
building.

Subordinate **adverb clauses** always begin with *adverbial conjunctions*. They are never unmarked. Check the following list to become familiar with some of the most common adverbial conjunctions.

ADVERBIAL CONJUCTIONS

after, although, as, as far as, as if, as long as, as soon as, as though, because, before, by the time, even if, even though, except, that, if, in case, in the event, in order that, now that, once, provided, rather than, since, so, so that, sooner than, though, till, until, when, where, while

EXERCISE SWE-15

Directions: Find and underline the **adverb clauses** in the following sentences (some sentences have more than one). Put parenthesis ( ) around the **main clauses**.

1. (Nielson ratings are used by television networks) <u>so that they know about a show's popularity</u>.

2. Garcia is the most common Latin last name, although Chang is the most popular last name in the world.

Remember that *since* has two meanings:
"क्यूंकि", "तब से (चूँकि)".

3. Even though no one knows the exact birth date of Jesus Christ, Christmas is celebrated around the world on December 25.

4. Since it was invented in 1886 the secret formula for making Coca Cola has been known to only seven men.

5. Because the ostrich is an extremely large bird, it cannot fly, although it can run at speeds of nearly 60 miles per hour.

6. Unless Robert repairs his bicycle he will have to take the bus to school, even though it will take him twice as much time.

7. Although Holland is the world's biggest producer of tulips, the flower actually came from Asia.

8. Until computers were invented, writers had to rely on typewriters even though their work was rather tedious.

9. The university bookstore will be closed this week so that inventory can be taken before the new semester begins.

10. Tickets for Broadway musicals are very expensive although half priced tickets are sometimes available if you wait until the last minute.

11. Please advise the front desk staff as soon as you know if you will be departing earlier than previously planned.

12. Unless our television is repaired by Saturday we won't be able to watch the football game.

13.   If you book your flight early you can qualify for dis-
       counts although any changes will be penalized.

14.   When his alarm clock rang Tony turned it off and con-
       tinued sleeping although it was time for him to wake
       up.

15.   The light of the moon can create a lunar rainbow, al-
       though its colors are weaker than those created by the
       sun.

We've now studied each type of subordinate clause individually and should be ready to work with them all together in complete sentences. In the following exercise we will practice distinguishing among **main clauses**, **subordinate clauses**, and
phrases. We'll further classify the subordinate clauses as
noun, adjective, or *adverb.*

Of course on the actual TOEFL exam you will not have to
actually classify sentences in this way. But understanding
these grammatical elements will improve your skills at identifying and correcting errors on the exam.

EXERCISE SWE-16

Directions: Examine the following sentences. If the underlined part is a **main clause**, write **MC** in the blank. Write **SC** for **subordinate clauses** and **(X)** for **phrases**. Further classify subordinate clauses by writing **(N)** for *noun*, **(ADJ)** for *adjective*, **(ADV)** for *adverb* above each one.

   _X_   1. Venezuela is located in the northeast corner of South America, <u>just above the equator</u>.

          2. Venezuela does not really experience changes in weather, <u>although the months of July and August are hotter than usual</u>.

          3. <u>A rainy season is experienced</u> from May to November.

          4. <u>Although many creeds are represented</u>, the majority of Venezuelans are Roman Catholic.

          5. Angel Falls, <u>which is the highest waterfall in the world</u>, is located in Venezuela.

          6. <u>Spanish is spoken in Venezuela</u>, although English is taught in the public school system.

          7. Nearly 50% of Venezuelans are under 18 years of age, <u>while 70% are under 30</u>.

          8. Like many Latin American countries, <u>Venezuela's police forces are generally undertrained, poorly paid, and understaffed</u>.

_____ 9. What changed Venezuela was the discovery of oil, which made it rich overnight.

_____ 10. Like Mexico City and Tokyo, Caracas has incredible traffic jams.

_____ 11. Venezuela has 144 miles of tropical beaches which includes 72 small islands.

_____ 12. That the Caracas subway system opened in 1983 has helped ease congestion in some parts of the city.

_____ 13. Until the bolivar was devalued in 1983, Caracas was one of the most expensive cities in the world.

_____ 14. That 75% of the population lives in an urban environment causes problems of overcrowded conditions.

_____ 15. Venezuela's Caribbean location makes it a paradise for many water sports, although some of the beaches near Caracas are polluted.

If you feel that you still need more practice in distinguishing among main clauses, subordinate clauses, and phrases, just pick up an English book, magazine, or newspaper. You'll find an endless supply of sentences just waiting to be studied.

Don't forget to ask yourself "what do I have?" and "what do I need?" when analyzing a TOEFL error. The following exercise will help you do just that. It contains sentences with a missing word. By looking at the structure of the sentence, try to decide what that missing word must be: **main subject** (subject of the main clause), **main verb** (verb of the main clause), **subordinating signal** (introductory word of the subordinate clause), or **subordinate verb** (verb of the subordinate clause). If you can work through this exercise with a clear understanding and few errors, you have successfully completed Step One and are ready to take your next step in the program.

EXERCISE SWE-17

Directions: One word has been omitted from the following sentences. In the blank, write the number that corresponds to the missing word: **1. main subject 2. main verb 3. subordinate signal 4. subordinate verb**

___2___ 1. Argentina _____ the second largest country in South America.

_____ 2. Argentina's capital is Buenos Aires, _____ is one of the largest cities in South America.

_____ 3. Many _____ visit Argentina, especially Buenos Aires.

_____ 4. People from many countries settled in Argentina, _____ most came from Spain and Italy.

_____ 5. Argentina's Constitution provides a government which _____ somewhat similar to that of the United States.

_____ 6. Unlike most other Latin American countries, _____ has relatively few Indians.

_____ 7. Argentine customs _____ the influence of immigrants from European countries.

_____ 8. Argentina has four main land regions, which _____ the Pampa, a grassy plain that extends 300 miles.

_____ 9. _____ enjoys four distinct seasons, much like those of the United States.

_____ 10. Buenos Aires has one of the busiest airports in Latin America, _____ some 200 other airports are located throughout the country.

_____ 11. Isabel Perón, _____ was the first woman to become president of a nation in the Western Hemisphere, was the wife of Juan Perón.

_____ 12. Argentina's economy _____ largely on agricultural products.

_____ 13. The nation _____ the world's leading exporter of beef.

_____ 14. The tango, which _____ in Buenos Aires, is an adaptation of a Spanish folk dance.

_____ 15. Many Argentines _____ Madonna's portrayal of Evita Perón in the movie adaption of Andrew Lloyd Webber's Broadway hit.

MINI TOEFL-5

Directions: In questions 1-5, choose the one word or phrase that best completes the sentence. In questions 6-10, identify the underlined word(s) that should be changed to correct the sentence. **TIME: 6 minutes**

_____ 1. Ducks have webbed feet that enable _____ swim fast, even in rough waters.

    (A) them to   (B) to their
    (C) its   (D) they

_____ 2. ⊙ _____ the ozone layer is completely destroyed, nearly all living creatures will die.

    (A) For   (B) So
    (C) Although   (D) If

⊙Note that in conditional sentences *is* is used with *will,* while *were* is used with *would.*

_____ 3. Although there is no cure for the common cold, sleeping, resting, _____ can be helpful.

(A) and to drink juice   (B) and drinking fluids
(C) and to drinking fluids (D) which drank fluids

_____ 4. _____ turns copper green is its patina, a green film.

(A) That   (B) What
(C) How   (D) What is

_____ 5. Crying _____ stress, although it may irritate the eyes.

(A) is relieving   (B) what they relieve
(C) relieves   (D) relieves it

_____ 6. New York City, which is one of the world's
                              A
largest cities, is larger than any other cities in the
   B   C   D
United States.

_____ 7. Although testing water samples, correct levels of
           A   B   C
chlorine can be maintained in swimming pools.
              D

_____ 8. After they became extinct, dinosaurs lived on the
           A   B   C
earth for nearly 150 million years.
                      D

_____ 9. <u>Since</u> Edward <u>was afraid</u> of <u>highs,</u> he <u>didn't join</u>
                A   B   C   D
his friends on the roller coaster ride.

_____ 10. <u>Although was</u> defeated for the <u>presidency,</u> Vice
               A   B
President Al Gore <u>was later</u> awarded the Nobel
                             C
Prize for his work <u>on</u> global warming.
                            D

POP QUIZ

Can you name the four definitions of the word *spring*?

What are the two meanings of *since*?

What is the difference between a main and subordinate clause?

What are the three types of subordinate clauses?

What are the five structures that function as subjects in English?

5-Step
TOEFL Prep
for Hindi Speakers

QUICK CHECK
Grammar Problem Areas

STEP ONE

MC	Main Clause
SC	Subordinate Clause

STEP TWO

> S=V	Subject-Verb Agreement
S=P	Subject-Pronoun Agreement
VTF	Verb Tense or Form
PFR	Pronoun Form or Reference

STEP THREE

VBL	Verbals
WF	Word Form

STEP FOUR

WO	Word Order
PS	Parallel Structure
UR	Unnecessary Repetition

STEP FIVE

CU	Correct Usage

Subject-Verb Agreement

Exercise SWE-18

Directions: Using the abbreviations that identify each type of error, classify the following ten errors, then try to correct the errors. Only ten of the twelve types of errors are listed.

PFR 1. We must remember to make us reservations early in order to secure accommodations during the holiday weekend.

VTF 2. Mark learned many new things by the time he finishes his TOEFL program.

CU   3. The French horn does a mellow tone that blends well with woodwind instruments.

UR   4. Simultaneously, both telephones rang at the same time.

MC   5. The boat floating down the river all afternoon.

S=V 6. The furniture in the apartment belong to the owner.

PS   7. The little boy aspires to be a race car driver, an astronaut, or a member of the fire department.

SC   8. The children remained sad, even though tried to cheer them up.

<u>VBL</u>   9. Although I am not a big fan of science fiction, the movie was quite interested.

<u>WF</u>   10. The lovely flowers at the wedding ceremony smelled sweetly and the candles softly glowed.

We begin **Step Two** with a study of subject-verb agreement. The concept of subject-verb agreement is quiet simple: singular subjects take singular verbs; plural subjects take plural verbs. Subject-verb agreement errors are fairly common on the TOEFL exam.

If you don't see an error immediately when taking Section Two of the TOEFL, first apply the information learned in Step One: divide the sentence, separating phrases, subordinate clauses, and the main clause (while checking for **MC** or **SC** errors). Then find the subject and verb in each clause and check for correct agreement.

We will examine several cases where the verb can be in either singular or plural form (depending on various factors), must always be in singular form, or must always be in plural form.

SINGULAR OR PLURAL VERBS

In the following cases, a singular or plural verb might be used depending on the structure of the sentence and the subject which the verb refers to.

1.   As you begin studying subject-verb agreement, concentrate on isolating the subject from phrases or clauses that
might separate the subject and verb. Prepositional phrases can
be especially tricky. Remember that words separating a subject
and verb have no effect on its singularity or plurality. Notice
the following example with prepositional phrases.

	accompanied by	
	together with	
The **teacher**	*as well as*	his students **is visiting** the museum.
	in addition to	
	along with	

You can see in this example that *the teacher* is **singular** and
the verb must also be **singular**. This is good subject-verb
agreement. Again, the phrase separating the subject and verb
have no effect. Often on the TOEFL exam a singular subject is
presented—followed by phrases containing many plural
words. By the time you get to the verb it sounds OK to put a
plural verb. Avoid this trap by isolating the subject.

2.   Collective nouns are words that refer to a group of
people. These words are almost always used in a singular
form. In fact, it sounds a bit rare to use them in a plural form.
However, for the TOEFL exam we must learn that it is indeed
possible to use such words in a plural form if it is considered
that *the individual members of the group are acting independently.* Some of these collective nouns include: *family, team,
police, class, audience, faculty,* etc.

How do we know if one of these words should take a singular or a plural verb? Simply check the sentence for a **pronoun** or **modifier** to give you reference. Compare the following sentences:

The *committee* **are** in the process of making **their** decisions.

The *committee* **is** in the process of making **its** decision.

3.   An easy rule to remember: nouns that refer to a language are singular but are plural when referring to a nationality. Compare the following:

Chinese **is** a difficult language to speak.

The *Chinese* **include** a great deal of rice in their diets.

4.   English includes some words that have Latin and Greek origins. These often have confusing singular and plural forms. Check the following list.

ध्यान दें कि अनुच्छेद *the* का उपयोग संज्ञा शब्दों जो किसी राष्ट्रीयता को दर्शाति हैं , के आगे होता है ।

SINGULAR	PLURAL
appendix	appendices
alumnus	alumni
basis	bases
criterion	criteria
datum	data
index	indices
medium	media
phenomenon	phenomena

5.   A few words in English do not change in form—they're the same in singular and plural. Some words always end in *s*, such as *series* and *species*. Other words, especially those referring to animals, never end in *s*, such as *sheep*, *deer*, *fish*, and *shrimp* (*fishes* and *shrimps* are alternative plural forms used in British English).

Check modifiers and pronouns for singular or plural reference. Compare the following:

Those shrimp **smell** delicious.

This **is** the last shrimp I can eat.

6. Words such as *none, all, some, half, majority, any,* etc., can be singular or plural, depending on what they refer to. If a prepositional phrase follows one of these words, check the object of the phrase to determine if it has singular or plural reference. Compare the following:

None of the **money** is mine.

None of the **guests** have arrived.

7. In their normal meanings, the words *there, here,* and *where* do not function as subjects. Sentences beginning with these words require an inversion of the subject and verb (see **WO** in Step Four). If your sentence begins with one of these words make sure the verb agrees with the subject, which is found *after* the verb. For example:

There **are** not enough books in the library.

Here **is** the message that was left for you this morning.

8. *Either...or, neither...nor,* and *not only...but also* are correlative conjunctions that introduce two subjects. The verb always agrees with the closer (second) subject. Examine the following:

Neither the children *nor* the **babysitter** likes the TV program.

Either the cats *or* the **dog** has destroyed the flower garden.

Not only the players *but also* the **coach** hopes for a victory.

Try this: Read the sentences again changing the position of the subjects (put the second subject first and the first one second) and change the verb to agree.

NOTE: these structures are also important when studying errors in pronoun-subject agreement (**S=P**, Step Two) and parallel structure (**PS**, Step Four). These simple structures can cause a wide variety of errors, but they're quite easy to learn. Learn them well—they could be worth several points on the TOEFL exam!

If you understand the above cases where a verb might be singular or plural in form, try the next exercise for practice.

EXERCISE SWE-19

Direction: Identify and underline the subjects of the following sentences. If the subject is *singular*, write **is** in the blank. If the subject is *plural*, write **are**.

1. <u>Cotton</u>, as well as wool and silk, __is__ produced from non-synthetic material.

2. The team _____ making plans for their big game.

3. The Japanese _____ known for technological advances.

Cotton is an example of an non-countable noun (just like *wool, silk, polyester, etc.*) Remember that non-countable nouns, by definition have no plural form—they couldn't possibly take a plural verb.

4. The data _____ now available for your reference.

5. Deer _____ sometimes cruelly hunted for their antlers.

6. All of the rooms in the hotel _____ reserved.

7. Here _____ the candles for the birthday cake.

8. Not only the flight attendants but also the pilots _____ planning to go on strike.

9. Alumni of the university _____ asked to make financial donations.

10. Ana, along with her sister and three brothers, _____ hoping to travel to Disney World.

11. English _____ spoken in nearly all parts of the world.

12. Here _____ the results of the medical tests.

13. Some of the tickets _____ still unsold.

14. The police _____ planning its annual fund-raising event.

15. All of the creeks _____ becoming polluted by the oil spill.

SINGULAR VERBS

Now we'll examine cases where a singular verb is always used.

1.   Titles of books, newspapers, magazines, etc. always take a singular verb (even if plural in form). Examine the following:

The New York Times **is** one of the most respected newspapers in the U.S.

Star Wars **has** been released again after many years.

2.   Academic subjects are always singular (even if plural in form). For example: 🌀 *mathematics, physics, statistics.* The same applies to certain sports activities such as *gymnastics.* Examine the following:

Mathematics **is** Robert's favorite subject.

Gymnastics **is** one of the most popular Olympic sports.

3.   Some abstract nouns such as *politics, news, ethics,* and *information* take singular verbs (even when plural in form). Examine the following:

🌀 Careful with this word. The word *mathematic* does not exist (it must end in *s* unless the shortened form *math* is used). Like all academic subjects, it is always singular in form.

Ethics **is** a branch of philosophy.

The *news* of the results **is** important to scientists.

Words like *news* can be tricky. While always ending in *s*, *news* is considered singular (and uncountable).

4.   Nouns indicating specific amounts or measurements of money, time, degree, or quantity take singular verbs. Examine the following:

Two hundred dollars **is** required to open a checking account.

Thirty minutes **isn't** enough time to finish my homework.

Can you think of similar sentences with this type of subject? Try now to formulate a few using various kinds of measurements.

5.   Names of diseases always take singular verbs (even when plural in form). For example, *measles, mumps, herpes, AIDS.* Examine the following:

 AIDS **is** preventable although proper education is necessary.

Measles **is** a serious disease for adults.

 Perhaps some difficult vocabulary here.
Measles means "खसरा ", *mumps* means "गल गण्ड रोग ", and
AIDS, which stands for Acquired Immune Deficiency Syndrome, means "एड्स ".

---

6.   The expression *the number of* takes a singular verb (*a number of* is plural). For example:

The number of students **is** increasing.

7.   Two subjects joined by *and* take a plural verb, but if preceded by *each* or *every* a singular verb is used.
Examine the following:

Each boy and girl **was** given a small gift at the party.

Every employee and visitor **wears** an identification tag.

8.   If the words *each, either,* or *neither* function as subjects, they take singular verbs. For example:

Each of those cars **has** been checked for mechanical problems.

9.   Words which end in "one", "body", or "thing" take singular verbs (even though they may be plural in meaning). These include words such as: *everyone, nothing, anybody, everything, nothing, someone,* etc.
For example:

Everybody at the conference **receives** a certificate.

Nothing **is** more important to a person's health than a proper diet.

10.   The introductory *it* takes a singular verb.
For example:

It **is** his lack of experience that makes him nervous about the new job.

Before we complete this **S=V** section, we'll take a break to complete a **MINI TOEFL** practice exercise. This will help you see how **S=V** errors might be tested in the TOEFL context. As always, some unrelated errors will be included.

The introductory *it* (sometimes referred to as the *impersonal, existential,* or *anticipatory it)* can be confusing. English teachers and grammar books often say that the *it* refers to "the fact". *It* really refers to nothing, but in English a verb must have a subject and if there is no subject we use *it* (avoid using *that* in its place).

MINI TOEFL-6

Directions: In questions 1-5, choose the one word or phrase that best completes the sentence. In questions 6-10 identify the underlined word(s) that should be changed to make the sentence correct. **TIME: 6 minutes**

_____ 1. Every partner and associate _____ invited to the seminar in order to become familiar with the latest advancements.

      (A) has been   (B) were
      (C) have been   (D) already

_____ 2. Mrs. Hall, along with her students and teaching assistants, _____ a trip to Europe this Summer.

      (A) will be   (B) are planning
      (C) were organizing   (D) is planning

_____ 3. Not only the crime rate, but also the percentage of unemployment, _____ taken into consideration when rating cities.

      (A) are   (B) had
      (C) is   (D) were

_____ 4. The criteria for accepting students in the new doctoral program _____ been established yet.

      (A) have not   (B) have
      (C) hasn't   (D) has also

_____ 5. A number of Mexican citizens _____ expressed outrage over the proposed U.S. immigration laws.

(A) has   (B) was
(C) have   (D) did

_____ 6. The information <u>on</u> the various dates and
                            A

<u>registration deadlines</u> <u>were</u> useful to <u>many</u> aspir-
         B   C   D

ing university students.

_____ 7. One of the <u>most famous</u> alumni of our university
                    A

he <u>was</u> asked <u>to speak</u> at the graduation.
B C   D

_____ 8. Matt, along with his classmates, <u>are planning</u> a
                            A

trip to Thailand <u>to celebrate</u> graduation
                 C

<u>from</u> medical school.
D

_____ 9. For decades, <u>studies</u> of cigarette smoking <u>have</u>
                A   B

shown that smoking is <u>extreme dangerous</u> and
                        C

<u>causes</u> cancer.
D

_____ 10. Although the researchers <u>are needing</u> addition-
                                       A

al funds to complete their project, the rector <u>has no</u>
                                             B

authority <u>to approve</u> <u>them</u>.
                 C   D

जारी रहने वाले वाक्यों में कुछ क्रियाओं का उपयोग मत करें | वो क्रिया जिनमें 'भाव' (पसंद, जरूरत, इच्छा, प्यार) व्यक्त होते हैं| यह कहना उचित है *I need money*, परन्तु *I am needing money* ठीक नहीं है |

PLURAL VERBS

In the following cases, a plural verb is always used.

1.   The expression *a number of* takes a plural verb (remember *the number of* takes a singular verb). For example:

A number of books **are** missing from the library.

2.   Two subjects joined by *and* take a plural verb (unless preceded by *each* or *every*). Examine the following:

Both the Ritz Hotel *and* the Plaza **are** completely booked this week.

A little boy *and* his mother **were** waiting for the school to open.

3.   Several, many, both and few take plural verbs. Examine the following:

Sometimes it is useful to make a mental association to help you remember rules and details needed for the TOEFL exam. Use your imagination. To remember these four words, for example, you might remember something like, "Sunday Morning BreakFast" to give you the starting letters of Several, Many, Both, and Few. Then imagine a picture that helps you relate your trigger words to the actual words you need to remember. In this case, you might imagine eggs for breakfast—several plates of eggs, one plate with many eggs, another with only a few, etc. It doesn't matter how ridiculous your mental picture is. In fact, the more unusual the idea, the more effective it is! A *few* of the classes **have** been relocated to other classrooms.

Both **are** hoping to qualify for scholarships that cover tuition.

4.   Many words that refer to articles of clothing or acces-
sories take plural verbs. Such words include: *shorts, pants,
jeans, trousers, glasses,* etc. They would take a singular verb,
however, if the subject were changed to *pair.* Compare the
following:

My sunglasses **are** black.

This *pair* of sunglasses **is** black.

5.   Many words describing tools take plural verbs. Such
words include: *tongs, scissors, pliers, tweezers, clippers,* etc.
Again, if you change the subject to *pair*, they take a singular
verb.

TWEEZERS   **PLIERS**

6.   Some words such as *riches, thanks,* and *means* always
take plural verbs unless the subject is changed with expressions such as *a word of, a note of, a world of,* etc.

We have now finished reviewing cases where a singular or plural verb is used, only a singular verb is used, or only a plural verb is used. Before we finish our study of **S=V** errors, we'll do some exercises that combine all of those situations.

EXERCISE SWE-20

Directions: Identify the subjects in the following sentences, then fill in the blank with **is** if the subject is singular or **are** if the subject is plural.

1. That species of bird __is__ common in Nebraska.

2. The baby deer in the zoo _____ playing with its mother.

3. The media _____ invited to cover the event.

4. Japanese _____ rarely studied by American students.

5. A number of teachers _____ attending the conference.

6. Mathematics _____ useful to engineers.

7. The faculty _____ discussing the parking problem among themselves.

8. Most of the money _____ mine.

9.   Not only the tulips but also the lilies _____ ⊙ bloom-
        ing.

10.   The towels and bed spreads _____ drying in the sun.

11.   Every car and truck _____ inspected to verify emis-
        sions.

12.   Here _____ the data you requested.

13.   It _____ the librarian who purchases the books.

14.   Everyone in the cast _____ an experienced singer or
        actor.

15.   The national news as well as local reports _____ dis-
        turbing.

EXERCISE SWE-21

Directions: Identify and underline the subject which the verb
must agree with. Then fill in the blanks with the correct verb
from the choices given at the end of the sentence.

1.   In its verdict, the <u>jury</u> __is__ finding the defendant
        innocent of all charges. (*is, are*)

⊙ *Blooming* comes from the verb *to bloom*: "खिलना" (फूलना).

2.   The history of indigenous languages _____ being stud-
      ied by the students in the comparative linguistics
      course. *(is, are)*

3.   Because of insufficient water treatment, cholera _____
      still a threat to those who don't consume only purified
      water. *(is, are)*

4.   For English speakers living in Seoul, *Essential Korean
      for Tourists* _____ phrases which are useful in daily
      communication. *(provides, provide)*

5.   Everyone in this group of musicians _____ a chance to
      be selected to perform in the concert. *(has, have)*

6.   Neither the sales manager nor the secretaries _____
      received their pay checks. *(has, have)*

7.   Soccer players and referees _____ protected from fans
      by a seven-foot moat which encircles the stadium in
      Rio de Janeiro. *(is, are)*

8.   There _____ a check for $300. in the envelope. *(was,
      were)*

9.   A blue and white van _____ waiting to take the execu-
      tives from the hotel to the airport. *(is, are)*

10.   Some of the movie _____ been cut to shorten its
      length to two hours. *(has, have)*

11.   Every parking attendant and usher _____ given free
      admission to the event in exchange for his volunteer
      work. *(is, are)*

12.   The number of crimes committed by juveniles _____ decreased substantially. *(has, have)*

13.   A good pair of sunglasses _____ essential for life-guards. *(is, are)*

14.   A school of tropical fish _____ seen by the scuba driver. *(was, were)*

15.   It _____ his athletic ability and his academic achievement that impressed the admissions officer. *(was, were)*

MINI TOEFL-7

Directions: In questions 1-5, choose the one word or phrase that best completes the sentence. In questions 6-10, identify the underlined word(s) that should be changed to correct the sentence. **Time: 6 minutes**

_____ 1. Every fruit and vegetable served by the restaurant _____ grown.

      (A) are organically   (B) were organically
      (C) have been organically   (D) is organically

_____ 2. Everyone, including the clerical staff, _____ to attend the staff meeting scheduled for tomorrow morning.

      (A) has   (B) will
      (C) have   (D) had

_____ 3. He was accepted by the university _____ .

(A) when he had seventeen years
(B) at the age of seventeen
(C) when seventeen were his age
(D) with seventeen years

_____ 4. Many students in Beijing as well as Tokyo _____ English classes and the TOEFL exam.

(A) assist   (B) takes
(C) take   (D) assists

_____ 5. My new screwdriver as well as a pair of pliers _____ found in the drawer.

(A) were   (B) had
(C) was   (D) also

_____ 6. All of the money which <u>were</u> discovered <u>in the</u>
                         A   B

thief's house <u>was believed</u> to be <u>counterfeit</u>.
                C   D

_____ 7. These bacteria <u>is sometimes</u> found in the
                        A

food supply but <u>can be</u> killed by <u>cooking</u> at a very
                 B   C

<u>high temperature</u>.
   D

Note: *counterfeit* is an adjective; it means *fake*,"नकली (कल्पित) ".

---

[87]

_____ 8. <u>The</u> Department of Foreign Languages <u>are</u> reque-
      A   B

sting <u>more funds</u> in order <u>to install</u> a sophisticated
            C   D

laboratory.

_____ 9. The president, <u>accompanied by</u> several secret ser-
                       A

vice agents and assistants, <u>are planning</u> <u>to arrive</u> to
                                    B   C

the press conference <u>within</u> minutes.
                          D

_____ 10. Not only the washer and dryer <u>but also</u> half of the
                                             A

furniture <u>have already</u> been <u>loaded</u> <u>onto</u> the mov-
                 B   C   D

ing truck.

POP QUIZ

How do you say *measles* and *mumps* in Hindi?

Is the word *furniture* singular or plural in form?

What is the singular form of the word *data*?

5-Step
TOEFL Prep
for Hindi Speakers

QUICK CHECK
Grammar Problem Areas

STEP ONE

MC	Main Clause
SC	Subordinate Clause

STEP TWO

S=V	Subject-Verb Agreement
> S=P	Subject-Pronoun Agreement
VTF	Verb Tense or Form
PFR	Pronoun Form or Reference

STEP THREE

VBL	Verbals
WF	Word Form

STEP FOUR

WO	Word Order
PS	Parallel Structure
UR	Unnecessary Repetition

STEP FIVE

CU	Correct Usage

Subject-Pronoun Agreement

EXERCISE SWE-22

Directions: Using the abbreviations that identify each type of error, classify the following ten errors, then try to correct the errors. Only ten of the twelve types of errors are listed.

WO   1. Rarely we do cook at home because we prefer eating out.

MC   2. German Shepherds, which make lovable pets, they are frequently trained to assist the blind.

PFR   3. The hair stylist whom does her hair is quite expensive.

S=V   4. Not only the teachers but also the principal have decided to play in the annual basketball game.

PS   5. When visiting New York, I enjoy shopping in So-Ho, attending Broadway plays, and to eat in China Town.

WF   6. *Avatar* was one of the expensivest movies ever produced.

VBL   7. Power surges aren't harmful to electrical appliances left unplugging.

S=P   8. Everyone leaving the concert must have their hand stamped in order to be readmitted.

UR   9. The brief, short report highlighted the most important events of the annual meeting of stockholders.

CU   10. Setting in the sun for long periods of time without any kind of protection can be harmful to the skin and could even cause cancer.

This program has been designed so that students can begin at any point, or skip around through the material as desired. However, if you've just finished studying the **S=V** (subject-verb agreement) point, the following **S=P** (subject-pronoun agreement) point will be easy. There are fewer rules and the rules are the same as the previous **S=V** rules. Subordination is still important when analyzing **S=P** errors; separate your clauses to correctly identify which pronoun refers to which subject, then check the agreement.

Before we begin our study of **S=P** errors, let's take a look at the various forms of pronouns. The following chart classifies all of the pronouns in English by their form (only the demonstrative pronouns, *this*, *that*, *these*, and *those* are not included). Refer often to this chart until the pronouns become familiar. This will also be important for the following **PFR** (pronoun form or reference) point.

QUICK CHECK

SUBJECT	OBJECT	POSSESSIVE ADJECTIVE	POSSESSIVE PRONOUN	REFLEX-IVE
I	ME	MY	MINE	MYSELF
YOU (SINGULAR)	YOU	YOUR	YOURS	YOURSELF
HE	HIM	HIS	HIS	HIMSELF
SHE	HER	HER	HERS	HERSELF
IT	IT	ITS	-----	ITSELF
WE	US	OUR	OURS	OUR-SELVES
YOU (PLURAL)	YOU	YOUR	YOURS	YOUR-SELVES
THEY	THEM	THEIR	THEIRS	THEM-SELVES
ONE	ONE	ONE'S	-----	ONESELF
WHO	WHOM	WHOSE	WHOSE	-----

The concept of subject-pronoun agreement is the same as that of subject-verb agreement. As mentioned, the rules are the same, but fewer. However, **S=P** errors can still be somewhat more difficult than **S=V** errors for one important reason: when checking the subject-verb agreement, there is only one singular or plural verb form from which to choose. But, when checking the subject-pronoun agreement, there are several singular choices from which to choose. We must think not only in number, but also 🌐 gender, form, and reference. Let's begin with a few examples of **S=P** errors. Try to find the subject-pronoun agreement errors in the following five sentences.

1.   Neither of the girls in my school has their own car.

2.   The coach as well as the players is in their office.

3.   Either Frank or Edward should have brought their watch.

4.   Each of the students has their credential.

5.   All of the library books have its own identification number.

🌐 याद रखे अंग्रेजी में व्यक्तिवाचक सर्वनाम का चुनाव करते समय वचन (एकवचन अथवा बहुवचन), लिंग (स्त्रीलिंग अथवा पुलिंग), न्यायसंगत हवाले का हमेशा ध्यान रखा जाता है ।

RULES FOR SUBJECT-PRONOUN AGREEMENT

1.   Words which end in "one", "body", or "thing", even though plural in meaning, take singular verbs (see rule number nine under "Singular Verbs".) Singular pronouns are also used to refer to these words.
For example:

Everybody at the conference receives **his** certificate today.

Everything should be put in **its** proper place.

2.   When two subjects are joined by *and* (unless preceded by *each* or *every*), a plural verb is required (see rule two under "Plural Verbs"). Plural pronouns are also used in this case.
For example:

Both Christine *and* Eloise are doing **their** homework

Peter *and* I are taking **our** cars.

Let's test our understanding of these two rules before continuing with the last two.

EXERCISE SWE-23

Directions: Identify the subjects and complete the sentences with an appropriate pronoun. Make sure to read the complete sentence and maintain logical reference.

1. Everyone who dines in this restaurant tonight will have __his__ parking ticket validated.

2. Both the cheerleaders and the football players will be issued _____ uniforms tomorrow.

3. Everyone is invited to bring _____ husband to the dinner.

4. Someone left _____ umbrella.

5. My cousin and I will spend _____ vacations in Hong Kong.

6. It is disturbing to the teacher that no one completed _____ final project on time.

7. Everyone should remain seated until _____ name is called.

8. Both snakes and iguanas shed _____ skin.

9. My sister and I are saving _____ money to buy a new computer.

10. Anyone who studies hard can improve _____ TOEFL score.

S=P RULES CONTINUED

3.   *Either...or, neither...nor*, and *not only...but also* are correlative conjunctions that introduce two subjects. The verb (see rule eight under "Singular or Plural Verbs") and the pronoun agree with the closest (second) subject. For example:

Either my mom *or* my **dad** left <u>his</u> keys on the table.

Not only the senators *but also* the **president** will give <u>his</u> speech tonight.

4.   Collective nouns (such as *family, team, police, class, audience, faculty,* etc.) can be used in a plural or singular form. If the verb is singular, use a singular pronoun. If the verb is plural, use a plural pronoun (see rule two under "Singular or Plural Verbs"). For example:

The *committee* **are** in the process of making **their** decisions.

The *committee* **is** in the process of making **its** decision.

Let's test our understanding of the final two rules by completing the following exercise.

EXERCISE SWE-24

Directions: Identify the subjects and complete the sentences with an appropriate pronoun.

1.   The crew is going to dock <u>its</u> ship tonight.

2.   Our team is trying to tie _____ previous record.

3.   Not only the captain but also the soldiers are in _____ camp.

4.   The family has moved to _____ new apartment.

5.   Either Janet or her sisters will take _____ turn next.

6.   The committee is going to present _____ report tomorrow.

7.   Neither the students nor the teachers have _____ class schedules.

8.   The faculty are preparing _____ recommendations.

9.   Neither the cats nor the dog is in _____ house.

10. Not only my brother but also my sister is finishing _____ degree.

Now let's combine all the rules for **S=V** and **S=P** and test our understanding with further practice. The following exercise is an excellent review of both subject-verb agreement and subject-pronoun agreement.

EXERCISE SWE-25

Directions: All of the following sentences are wrong because they have errors in subject-verb agreement and/or subject-pronoun agreement. Rewrite the sentences, correcting the errors.

1. Neither the reporters nor the photographer have received their assignment.

    Neither the reporters nor the photographer **has** received **his** assignment.

2. Everyone have to present their identification in order to receive a discount.

    _____

    _____

3. The English department, along with the other departments, are going to order their new computer equipment soon.

    _____

    _____

4.   The one million dollars were given to the lucky winner who won them in the raffle.

_____

_____

5.   Both Orlando and San Francisco is popular in the winter because of its warm weather.

_____

_____

6.   The catalog listing U.S universities are available at the library because many students request them.

_____

_____

7.   Anyone who abuses their pet should be criminally charged for their actions.

_____

_____

8.   Everyone need to take their final exam today.

_____

_____

9.   Many a man have tried to discover the fountain of youth.

_____

_____

10.   Contrary to speculation, books has actually increased in popularity in our computer age; many thought it would disappear.

_____

_____

Before we continue our study of other verb and pronoun errors, let's end this section with a **MINI TOEFL** practice exercise.

MINI TOEFL-8

Directions: In questions 1-5, choose the one word or phrase that best completes the sentence. In questions 6-10, identify the underlined word(s) that should be changed to correct the sentence. **Time: 6 minutes**

_____   1. *The New York Times,* famous for _____ Sunday edition, features critiques of Broadway musicals.

            (A) their   (B) it's
            (C) his   (D) its

_____ 2. Unlike any other U.S. president, President Clinton
         believed it to be in the best interest of _____ coun-
         try to fight the tobacco companies.

         (A) their   (B) her
         (C) his   (D) its

_____ 3. That chain of fast food restaurants will go out of
         business if it doesn't find a way to improve _____

         (A) its hamburgers   (B) it's hamburgers
         (C) their hamburgers   (D) our hamburgers

_____ 4. Not only the doctor but also the nurses are attend-
         ing _____ patients in the emergency room.

         (A) his   (B) her
         (C) them   (D) their

_____ 5. Everyone must bring _____ final project to class
         today.

         (A) its   (B) his
         (C) my   (D) their

_____ 6. Both the lawyer and <u>his</u> clients <u>are required</u> by law
                              A   B
         to present <u>his</u> case before the <u>grand jury</u> on
                    C   D
         Wednesday.

_____ 7. <u>Although</u> it is <u>illegal,</u> some people <u>still throw</u> <u>his</u>
              A   B   C   D
         trash out of the car window.

_____ 8. Everyone <u>have</u> to be at <u>his</u> job no later <u>than</u> 8:00
                          A   B   C
        <u>tomorrow morning.</u>
                D

_____ 9. The <u>Japanese</u> soccer team is preparing <u>for</u> <u>their</u>
                      A   B   C
        important World Cup game <u>against</u> the undefeated
                                              D
        Brazilian team.

_____ 10. <u>Not only</u> the panda but also the polar bears <u>will be</u>
                  A   B
        moved from <u>its</u> homes in the zoo to a <u>warmer</u> cli-
                        C   D
        mate.

5-Step
TOEFL Prep
for Hindi Speakers

QUICK CHECK
Grammar Problem Areas

STEP ONE

MC	Main Clause
SC	Subordinate Clause

STEP TWO

S=V	Subject-Verb Agreement
S=P	Subject-Pronoun Agreement
> VTF	Verb Tense or Form
PFR	Pronoun Form or Reference

STEP THREE

VBL	Verbals
WF	Word Form

STEP FOUR

WO	Word Order
PS	Parallel Structure
UR	Unnecessary Repetition

STEP FIVE

CU	Correct Usage

Verb Tense or Form

Time Markers

Irregular Verbs

EXERCISE SWE-26

Directions: Using abbreviations that identify each type of error, classify the following ten errors, then try to correct the errors. Only ten of the twelve types of errors are listed.

S=P 1. Both Chandak and Chandan are doing his homework.

VTF 2. The club president will led tonight's discussion on upcoming community projects.

CU 3. The team doctor has all ready rushed to the sidelines to examine the injured player.

WO 4. Under the table three boxes of books are.

SC 5. Mexico City has been testing an alarm system will alert residents of earthquakes approaching from the Pacific coast.

UR 6. Due to rising coast of paper, the prices of books have increased by nearly 25% more.

VBL 7. Jonathon and I are very interested in the apartment advertising in today's paper.

S=V 8. Either the Amazon or the Nile are the world's longest river.

PS   9.   *Carmen, The Barber Of Seville,* and the music of *The Marriage of Figaro* are popular among opera fans.

MC   10.   Playing ping-pong it is good exercise for violinists.

While subject-verb agreement is important, it is also important to spend a little time reviewing the **tense** and **form** of verbs (**VTF** errors). It might be useful to also review the reference appendices **A. Irregular verbs** and **F. Verb Tense Models** in the Appendices.

We'll begin with tense errors. These errors involve **time markers** which control the verb tense. A time marker can be a word or phrase that specifies the time—the verb should be in logical agreement with the time marker. This is grammatical, but also logical. 🌐 You would not want to say that you *did* something *tomorrow*, or that you're *going to do* something *yesterday*.

If your **time marker** clearly indicates *past activity*, make sure your verb is in a past tense. If your time marker indicates *future activity*, make sure your verb is in a future tense. If your time marker indicates that the subject of the sentence is *dead*, make sure your verb is "*dead*". In other words don't use an active verb with a dead subject.

🌐 "आने वाले कल में मैंने कुछ किया था" अथवा "बीत चुके कल में कुछ करने जा रहा हूँ" ।

Most students do not have great difficulty in using correct tenses with time markers. There are, however, two groups of **"special" time markers** that might cause confusion. The first group includes time markers such as: *up until now…, for some time now…, since…, so far…* All of these time markers have the same basic meaning: *"until this moment in time"*.

समय के एस समय तक

They indicate that an activity has started in the past, continued into the present, but without completion—the activity continues.

When you have a time marker indicating this type of activity you'll need to use the **present perfect** or **present perfect continuous tense**. The formula for constructing the **present perfect** tense is:

has / have + participle

The formula for constructing the **present perfect continuous** tense is:

has / have + been + present participle

For example:

Ana has been studying for the TOEFL *since last month.*

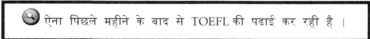 ऐना पिछले महीने के बाद से TOEFL की पढाई कर रही है ।

The time marker in this sentence is *since last month,* which indicates present perfect activity. Notice *has* is used because *Ana* is singular (*have* is used for plural subjects).

The second group includes time markers that begin with *by,* such as: *by the end of this year* and *by this time next year.* These mark a specified time in the future in order to speculate about completed activity *by* a certain time.

इस वर्ष के अंत तक ....अगले वर्ष इस समय तक ।

These types of time markers are used to speculate about past, completed activity in the future. The activity has not been completed at this moment in time, but will be completed *by* a certain time. *From a point of view in the **present** you're speculating about **completed** activity in the **future**.*

When you have a time marker indicating this type of activity you'll need to use the **future perfect** or **future perfect continuous tense**. The formula for constructing the **future perfect** tense is:

will + have + past participle

The formula for constructing the **future perfect continuous** tense is:

will + have + been + present participle

For example: Ana will have learned many things *by the end of the class.*

 ऐना ने क्लास के अंत तक कई चीजें सीख ली होंगी ।

The time marker in this sentence is *by the end of the class,* which indicates future perfect activity. Notice there is no distinction between singular and plural; *have* is always used, not *has.* Also, only the *past participle* (not the present participle) is used.

EXERCISE SWE-27

Directions: Underline the time markers and put parentheses ( ) around the verbs in the following sentences. If the verb is in the correct tense write **OK** in the blank. If the verb is in the wrong tense put an **X**.

 OK   1. <u>From time to time</u> every car (needs) a tune up.

_____ 2. The government is planning for some time now to devalue its currency.

_____ 3. The stadium is under reconstruction since the end of the football season.

_____ 4. So far no decisions have been reached concerning the proposal.

_____ 5. No solution has been found up until now.

_____ 6. When she died, Princess Diana has been in her thirties.

_____ 7. By the end of the class most students will had finished the assignment.

_____ 8.   In the early seventies, Donna Summer is recording numerous disco hits.

_____ 9.   The temperature has been dropping quickly since this morning.

_____ 10. By the time we get home the guests will had arrive for the birthday party.

That concludes our work on verb tense. Now we'll continue our **VTF** study by working with verb form errors. As you know, many verbs in English have irregular past and past participle forms—it might be useful to refer to Appendix A. It is necessary that you have a good working knowledge of these irregular verb forms.

It will be useful to begin reviewing these if you don't know them well. Besides reviewing lists, it might be helpful to make flash cards or listen to recordings of irregular forms. This is, unfortunately, a question of rote memorization. There is no magical way to learn them. Some grammar books categorize these verbs into groups that follow certain spellings. This might only make matters more confusing.

EXERCISE SWE-28

Directions: All of the following sentences are incorrect. Circle the verb that is in the wrong tense and write the correct verb in the blank.

made 1. Global communications have been (make) easier thanks to e-mail.

_____ 2. The first triathlon was hold in Hawaii in February, 1978.

_____ 3. Dick Francis has wrote many books with a horse-racing theme.

_____ 4. In general, cats will lived longer than dogs.

_____ 5. Tattoos, while offensive to some, have became quite popular.

_____ 6. It was recently discovering that there are ice formations on the moon.

_____ 7. The longest symphony, Number Three in D Minor, was wrote by Gustav Mahler.

_____ 8. A good upholsterer can made an old couch just like new.

_____ 9. The development of electric cars has gave new hope for reducing air pollution.

_____ 10. This pocket watch was give to me by my great grandfather.

_____ 11. Only 1,116 Stradivarius violins were make, of which some 700 can be accounted for today.

_____ 12. Jupiter is know as the largest planet in our solar system.

_____ 13. The postman was bit by the ferocious dog.

_____ 14. At the trial, the defendant sworn to tell the truth.

_____ 15. For several hours, no one knew what had became of the lost child.

Before we continue our study of other pronoun errors, let's end this section with a **MINI TOEFL** practice exercise.

MINI TOEFL-9

Directions: In questions 1-5, choose the one word or phrase that best completes the sentence. In questions 6-10, identify the underlined word(s) that should be changed to correct the sentence. **Time 6 minutes**

_____ 1. For some time now, cigarette advertising _____ tightly controlled by the United States government.

　　　(A) has been　　　(B) have been
　　　(C) was　　　　　(D) is

_____ 2. Hana _____ her doctorate by the end of next year.

    (A) will have finished   (B) will has finished
    (C) has finished   (D) finished

_____ 3. The book club _____ a new book during the first week of each month.

    (A) always sending   (B) always send
    (C) always   (D) always sends

_____ 4. The choir director will _____ the presentation of Handel's *Messiah*.

    (A) led   (B) lead
    (C) leads   (D) have lead

_____ 5. My sister has _____ quite fluent in Spanish while living in Chile.

    (A) become   (B) became
    (C) becoming   (D) having become

_____ 6. <u>Many</u> of the passengers that <u>were killed</u> in the air-
     A   B
plane crash <u>are flying</u> to Tokyo <u>to attend</u> a confer-
             C   D
ence on business administration.

_____ 7. After the <u>mischievous</u> little boy <u>had threw</u> a rock
              A   B
through the <u>neighbor's</u> window he was <u>severely</u>
             C   D
punished by his parents.

_____ 8. Steven Spielberg <u>has became</u> one of the <u>most</u>
                                A   B
popular film <u>directors</u> in the U.S.
   C   D

_____ 9. Although the development of the <u>artificial</u> lan-
                                                       A
guage Esperanto <u>was an</u> <u>extreme important</u>
                        B   C
achievement, it <u>no longer remains</u> very popular.
                            D

_____ 10. The <u>incredibly advance</u> of English across the <u>face</u>
                        A   B
of the globe is a <u>phenomenon</u> without parallel <u>in</u>
                        C   D
the history of language.

POP QUIZ

Can you translate the following sentences into English?

जॉन तीन सप्ताह से TOEFL की पढाई कर रहा है ।
मैरी कक्षा के समाप्त होने से पहले कई
नई चीज़ें सीख चुकी होगी ।

Do you know the past and past participle forms of these verbs?

Become

Swing

Swear

Begin

Lose

Feel

Fall

5-Step TOEFL Prep

for Hindi Speakers

QUICK CHECK
Grammar Problem Areas

STEP ONE

MC	Main Clause
SC	Subordinate Clause

STEP TWO

S=V	Subject-Verb Agreement
S=P	Subject-Pronoun Agreement
VTF	Verb Tense or Form
> PFR	Pronoun Form or Reference

STEP THREE

VBL	Verbals
WF	Word Form

STEP FOUR

WO	Word Order
PS	Parallel Structure
UR	Unnecessary Repetition

STEP FIVE

CU	Correct Usage

Pronoun Form or Reference

EXERCISE SWE-29

Directions: Using the abbreviations that identify each type of error, classify the following ten errors, then try to correct the errors. Only ten of the twelve types of errors are listed.

PS   1. Among the qualities desired of the new director are patience, reliability, and to be punctual.

CU   2. Beside a Corvette, Daniel also owns a Mercedes and a Ferrari.

PFR   3. The teacher doesn't approve of us speaking Hindi in our English class.

S=P   4. Carmen and I will spend my weekend at the beach.

WF   5. The teacher kept the student's attention with a real interesting story.

S=V   6. Mathematics are difficult for me, although I enjoy studying algebra.

SC   7. The Howrah Bridge which is located in Calcutta, India which is the world's busiest bridge.

VTF   8. By the end of the day the box office will sold all of the tickets for the concert.

WO   9. Only once I have been to Disneyland.

VBL   10. The press was extremely interested in the president's interested news conference.

Now we return to pronouns to complete STEP TWO with a study of errors in pronoun form and reference (**PFR** errors). Hopefully you're already familiar with the various forms of pronouns after reviewing the chart at the start of the **S=P** section. Let's review the chart again, this time as an exercise to test your memory. If you haven't studied the **S=P** section, take a quick look at the pronoun chart before continuing.

EXERCISE SWE-30

Directions: Some blanks have been left in the following chart of pronoun forms. Fill in the blanks with the correct pronoun form. Check your work with the complete chart on page 96.

SUBJECT	OBJECT	POSSESSIVE ADJECTIVE	POSSESSIVE PRONOUN	REFLEX-IVE
I	ME	_____	MINE	MYSELF
YOU(SINGULAR)	YOU	YOUR	YOURS	_____
HE	HIM	HIS	———	HIMSELF
SHE	_____	HER	HERS	HERSELF
IT	IT	_____	-----	ITSELF
WE	US	_____	OURS	OUR-SELVES
YOU(PLURAL)	YOU	YOUR	_____	YOUR-SELVES
THEY	_____	THEIR	THEIRS	THEM-SELVES
ONE	ONE	ONE'S	-----	_____
_____	WHOM	WHOSE	WHOSE	-----

Be careful with a few confusing elements of the pronoun organization. Notice that the possessive adjective and pronoun for *he* are the same: *his*. However, the object and possessive adjective for *she* are the same: *her*, while the possessive pronoun is different. Also be careful with the possessive adjective *its*. Notice there is no apostrophe. Adding the apostrophe completely changes the meaning of the word: *it's* is the contraction of the verb *to be*, "it is".

In informal English you might hear some incorrect pronoun forms. Avoid using incorrect forms such as *hisself* or *theirselves*.

Should you have difficulty keeping the various forms straight, it might be useful to remember a simple sentence as an example of each form.

Note the following example sentences (abbreviations for the respective forms are used):

I (S) sing a song.

She sings a song to **me** (O).

This is **my** (PA) book.

This book is **mine** (PP).

I cooked dinner **myself** (R).

मैं गाना गाता हूँ ।
वो मेरे लिए गाना गाती है ।
यह मेरी किताब है ।
यह किताब मेरी है ।
मैंने रात का खाना स्वयं बनाया ।

Let's practice with the various pronoun forms. Continue referring to your chart of pronoun forms until you are confident of
using them correctly. Substitute forms using your example
sentences if necessary. Also remember that subordination is
important here—you must identify clauses in order to correctly
identify pronoun forms.

EXERCISE SWE-31

Directions: Using the abbreviations for the pronoun forms (S,
O, PA, PP, R), identify the underlined pronoun forms in the
following sentences by putting the correct abbreviation in the
blank.

__S__   1. <u>He</u> is the owner of that beautiful new home.

_____   2. That beautiful new home belongs to <u>him</u>.

_____   3. That is <u>his</u> beautiful new home.

_____   4. That beautiful new home is <u>his</u>.

_____   5. He bought the beautiful new home <u>himself</u>.

_____   6. It was <u>she</u> who made the decision.

_____   7. This is a photograph of Angie and one of <u>her</u>
friends.

_____   8. Your TOEFL score is much higher than <u>mine</u>.

_____   9. <u>Your</u> singing is hurting my ears!

_____ 10. <u>Whom</u> did you visit on your trip to Costa Rica?

_____ 11. The girl <u>who</u> came to my party was beautiful.

_____ 12. The cat is in <u>its</u> house.

_____ 13. We must send <u>our</u> college admission applications this week.

_____ 14. Christopher taught <u>himself</u> to speak Portuguese.

_____ 15. <u>It</u> was the biggest birthday cake I had ever seen.

Before we begin our study of the rules for each pronoun form, let's stop and do a **MINI TOEFL** practice exercise. NOTE: In this exercise, unlike other similar exercises, *all* of the errors are related to pronoun form. We'll repeat this exercise after reviewing the pronoun form rules, so don't worry if you have a few errors the first time.

MINI TOEFL-10

Directions: In questions 1-5, choose the one word or phrase that best completes the sentence. In questions 6-10, identify the underlined word(s) that should be changed to make the sentence correct. **TIME: 6 minutes**

_____ 1. Although the voice sounds familiar, I'm not completely sure _____ is on the phone.

    (A) who   (B) whose
    (C) whom   (D) it's

_____ 2. Everyone except _____ was invited to the party.

    (A) hers   (B) she
    (C) her   (D) herself

_____ 3. If you were _____, would you allow Terri to go to the concert?

    (A) me   (B) her
    (C) my   (D) I

_____ 4. Our parents don't approve of _____ staying out past midnight.

    (A) our   (B) we
    (C) us   (D) ours

_____ 5. Instead of spending money on a hotel room, I think I'll stay with some friends of _____ when I go to visit Lima.

(A) me   (B) I
(C) our   (D) mine

_____ 6. The man <u>whom</u> lives above <u>my</u> apartment disturbs
               A   B
<u>me</u> with <u>his</u> extremely loud music.
C   D

_____ 7. After asking <u>it residents</u> to conserve water <u>during</u>
                 A   B
the drought, the city government <u>was</u> finally
                                            C
forced to <u>shut off</u> the water for 24 hours.
            D

_____ 8. <u>Because</u> the play required several quick <u>costume</u>
          A   B
changes, the actors had to dress <u>theirselves</u> very
                                     C
quickly <u>between acts</u>.
        D

Drought means "सूखा" while **flood** means "बाढ़". It's interesting that *drought* is a non-countable noun while *flood* is a countable noun.

_____ 9. Between <u>you and I</u>, I think Patricia is gaining
                  A
weight <u>because</u> she has <u>little time</u> for exercise <u>with</u>
           B   C   D
her full schedule of classes.

_____ 10. I <u>don't mind</u> sharing <u>me</u> lunch <u>with you</u>, but <u>I only</u>
            A   B   C   D
brought peanut butter crackers.

Note: In the above questions number 3 and 9, you'll find two very common errors. In informal speech, even native speakers will say "between you and *I*" and "if you were *me*". The correct forms are: "between you and *me*" and "if you were *I*". The rules that follow will explain why.

RULES FOR PRONOUN FORM

Remember, when you have an error in pronoun form it's because you're using the *incorrect* form. If you apply the following rules for the five forms of pronouns, you should be able to avoid such errors.

SUBJECT PRONOUNS

Subject pronouns include *I, you, he, she, we* etc. Keep referring to your pronoun form chart until you can remember them. Also keep in mind that the following three subject pronoun rules apply to the correct use of *who*.

1.   Our first rule is quite logical. Use a subject pronoun if the pronoun is functioning as a subject. It could be the subject of the main or subordinate clause.

अगर सर्वनाम एक विषय की तरह काम कर रहा हो तो एक विषय सर्वनाम का उपयोग करना चाहिए । ये प्रधान उपवाक्य अथवा गौण उपवाक्य का विषय हो सकता है।

Many people, even native speakers of English, have trouble with the use of *who* and *whom*. Remember that *who* is the subject form, and its use follows the subject pronoun rules, while *whom* is an object form and its use follows the object pronoun rules. Some English grammar books might give you special rules for the use of *who* and *whom*. This is really not necessary, however. You probably don't have much trouble with other subject or object forms such as *I* and *me* or *he* and *him*. If you get confused with *who* or *whom* try substituting it with a pronoun that is easier for you (if you would use *I*, use *who*, if you would use *me*, use *whom*, for example).

Notice the subject pronouns in the following examples:

He watched a movie on TV after his parents went to bed.

After *he* went to bed, his parents watched a movie.

2.   Use a subject pronoun form immediately following any form of the verb *to be*.

> किसी भी तरह की क्रिया *to be* के बाद विषय सर्वनाम के उपयोग करना चाहिए ।

Notice the subject pronouns in the following examples:

It was **he** at the door.

It must have been **they** who called last night.

3.   Use a subject pronoun form when comparing two subjects (avoid mixing subject and object forms).

> किन्ही दो वस्तुओं की तुलना करते समय विषय सर्वनाम का उपयोग करना चाहिए (उद्देश्य और विधेय का आपस में मिलाना नहीं चाहिए) ।

Notice the subject pronouns in the following examples:

They studied for their exam more than **we** did.

She is much taller than **I**.

EXERCISE SWE-32

Directions: Examine the subject pronouns in the following sentences. If the sentences are correct, write **OK** in the blank. If they are incorrect, put an (**X**).

_**X**_   1. If you were me, would you wear a coat and tie to the party?

_____   2. The neighbors whom live across the street are very nice.

_____   3. It might have been she who wrote you the secret letter.

_____   4. Henry has more computer experience than I.

_____   5. Y'all must be quiet in the library.

_____   6. They have practiced more for the game than us.

_____   7. The criminal whom the police arrested was recently convicted.

_____   8. If I were you, I would try to get more rest.

_____   9. She has saved more money for the trip than I.

_____ 10. When she first moved her didn't know anyone.

OBJECT PRONOUNS

Object pronouns include: *me, her, him, us, them,* etc. These rules apply to the correct use of *whom*.

1.   This rule is like the first rule for the subject form. Use an object pronoun if the pronoun is functioning as an object (direct or indirect).

अगर सर्वनाम वाक्य (प्रधान अथवा गौण) में विधेय (प्रत्यक्ष /अप्रत्यक्ष) की तरह काम करता हो तो वस्तुवाचक सर्वनाम का उपयोग करना चाहिए ।

Notice the object pronouns in the following examples:

If I buy **him** a drink, he will be very happy.

That woman is staring at **me**.

2.   Use an object pronoun when the pronoun functions as the object of a preposition. A list of prepositions is found in the Appendices. Prepositions include words such as: *between, among, with, but, except.*

अगर सर्वनाम पूर्वसर्ग के विधेय की तरह काम कर रहा हो तो वस्तुवाचक सर्वनाम का उपयोग करना चाहिए ।

Notice the object pronouns in the following examples:

Everyone except **her** was invited to the party.

The girl with **whom** I live is my sister.

3.   This rule is similar to the third rule for the subject form. Use an object pronoun when comparing two objects.

दो वस्तुओं की तुलना करते समय वस्तुवाचक सर्वनाम का उपयोग करना चाहिए ।

Notice the object pronouns in the following examples:

The teacher likes **you** better than **me**.

The puppy plays more with **me** than with **her**.

EXERCISE SWE-33

Directions: Examine the object pronouns in the following sentences. If the sentences are correct, write **OK** in the blank. If they are incorrect, put an (**X**).

___X___ 1. This secret must be kept strictly confidential between you and I.

_____ 2. Our guests, whom are visiting from Germany, will leave tomorrow.

_____ 3. If I see her at the party tonight I'll tell her to call you.

_____ 4. I'll be mad if you go to the movie without me.

_____ 5. No one except the teacher knows whom passed the test.

_____ 6. If you want to go with I, you'd better get ready fast.

_____ 7. The doctor is more concerned about my sister than me.

_____ 8. If you buy him the CD, he will be happy.

_____ 9. The friend whom I called was not at home.

_____ 10. The babysitter seems to like my sister more than I.

POSSESSIVE ADJECTIVES

Possessive adjectives include: _my, your, his, her, our, their,_ etc. We have only two rules for this form.

1.   Use the possessive adjective form to modify a noun and indicate possession.

> किसी संज्ञा को बदलने और इसपर अधिकार व्यक्त करने के लिए स्वत्वबोधक विशेषण का उपयोग करना चाहिए ।

Notice the object pronouns in the following examples:

This is **my** book.

This is **your** book.

These are **our** books.

2.   The possessive adjective form is used to modify a gerund. Careful here! It might sound good to put an object form in this position and you will often hear it incorrectly spoken.

> स्वत्वबोधक विशेषण का उपयोग क्रियावाचक संज्ञा को बदलने के लिए भी किया जाता है।

Notice the possessive adjectives in the following examples:

She appreciates **my** helping her.

The child loves **her** reading bedtime stories to him.

EXERCISE SWE-34

Directions: Examine the possessive adjectives in the following sentences. If the sentences are correct, write OK in the blank. If they are incorrect, put an (**X**).

  OK   1.   That dog seems to have lost its way home.

_____ 2.   Does my violin playing bother you?

_____ 3. Anne Rice demonstrates a great deal of imagination in her novels.

_____ 4. This is not mine book.

_____ 5. The preacher is bothered by us speaking during the church service.

_____ 6. Your problem should be checked by a medical professional.

_____ 7. My brother is jealous of my winning the scholarship.

_____ 8. You selling the car so quickly comes as a surprise.

_____ 9. Her dog bit her three times on her leg.

_____ 10. Please write your names on your answer sheets.

POSSESSIVE PRONOUNS

Possessive pronouns include: *mine, yours, hers, his, ours, theirs*, etc. We have three rules for the use of this form.

1.   The possessive pronoun form is used to avoid repeating a noun which functions as the subject or object of a main clause or to avoid repeating the second noun in a comparison (a comparison of similar things with different owners).

स्वत्वबोधक सर्वनाम का उपयोग वाक्य में संज्ञा को बार बार इस्तेमाल न करने के लिए किया जाता है । संज्ञा जो प्रधान वाक्य में उददेश्य या विधेय की तरह काम करती है . उसे दूसरे उददेश्य से अलग दिखने के लिए भी स्वत्वबोधक सर्वनाम का उपयोग किया जाता है । (जैसे कि दो समान वस्तुएं जिनके मालिक अलग अलग हों)

This rule might seem somewhat complicated, but should be easier after examining the following examples:

He forgot his book so he borrowed **mine**.

My girlfriend is prettier than **yours**.

Your test grade is high but **hers** isn't.

My sister's car is larger than **mine**.

2.　　You can use the possessive pronoun form with the verb *to be* to show possession.

स्वत्वबोधक सर्वनाम का उपयोग क्रिया *to be* के साथ अधिकार दिखाने के लिए किया जा सकता है ।

Notice the possessive pronouns in the following examples:

This sweater is **his**.

These flowers are **hers**.

3. You can also use the possessive pronoun form with the preposition *of* to show possession.

स्वत्वबोधक सर्वनाम का उपयोग पूर्वसर्ग *of* के साथ अधिकार दिखाने के लिए किया जा सकता है ।

Notice the possessive pronouns in the following examples:

This is an old book *of* **mine**.

I would like you to meet some friends *of* **ours**.

EXERCISE SWE-35

Directions: Examine the possessive pronouns in the following sentences. If the sentences are correct, write **OK** in the blank. If they are incorrect, put an (**X**).

<u> X </u> 1. Maya and a friend of her will meet us at the air-port.

_____ 2. Your grades are good but mine are not.

_____ 3. Your collection of compact disks is much bigger than my.

_____ 4. The clothes in the dryer are ours.

_____ 5. I found an old composition of her in the box in the attic.

_____ 6. Ralph's ideas are very different from mine.

_____ 7. I think this umbrella is your because that one is mine.

_____ 8. These books are not ours; they are property of the library.

_____ 9. You car is much faster than his.

_____ 10. Your apartment is perfectly clean while mine is a disaster.

REFLEXIVE PRONOUNS

The last group of pronouns that we will study is the reflexive form. This is probably the easiest group to learn. Reflexive pronouns include: _myself, himself, ourselves,_ etc. Study the following three rules.

1. The reflexive form is used (optionally) to emphasize a noun or pronoun which refers to people.

> बाध्य विधि का उपयोग, संज्ञा और सर्वनाम के उन शब्दों को, जो इन्सानों से संबंधित हो, को महत्व देने के लिए किया जाता है ।

Notice the reflexive pronouns in the following examples:

Michael Jordan **himself** autographed my basketball.

Since I live alone, I do all the housecleaning **myself.**

2.	The reflexive form is used with the preposition *by* to indicate that someone or something does an activity alone or without help.

बाध्य विधि का उपयोग अनुच्छेद *by* के साथ किया जाता है तो यह व्यक्त करता है की किसी ने कुछ स्वयं या किसी की सहायता के बिना किया है ।

For example:

The timid girl prefers to be *by* **herself**.

Oliver learned to play the violin *by* **himself**.

3.	The reflexive form is used when a person receives bodily harm.

बाध्य विधि का उपयोग तब किया जाता है जब इंसान को शारीरिक क्षति पहुंची हो ।

Here, you *hurt, cut,* or *burn* **yourself**.

For example:

Don't burn **yourself** with those matches!

Carol hurt **herself** while skating down the steep hill.

EXERCISE SWE-36

Directions: Examine the reflexive pronouns in the following sentences. If the sentences are correct, write **OK** in the blank. If they are incorrect, put an (**X**).

___X___ 1. My brother always gets hisself in difficult situations.

_____ 2. The president itself will give the commencement address.

_____ 3. We enjoy making home improvements ourselves.

_____ 4. Edward taught himself to play tennis.

_____ 5. Our daughter is too young to stay home by herself.

_____ 6. Be careful not to cut yourself on the broken glass.

_____ 7. The students themselves planned the homecoming parade.

_____ 8. I enjoy travelling by yourself.

_____ 9. I painted the bedroom myself.

_____ 10. Jack and Jill are enjoying theirselves on vacation.

Before we complete the **PFR** section with a short study of pronoun reference, let's repeat the MINI TOEFL practice exercise that we did before we studied the individual rules for pronoun form. Remember, *all* of the errors are related to pronoun form. This time, you should be able to complete the exercise without any errors.

MINI TOEFL-11

Directions: In questions 1-5, choose the one word or phrase that best completes the sentence. In questions 6-10, identify the underlined word(s) that should be changed to make the sentence correct. **Time: 6 minutes**

_____ 1. Although the voice sounds familiar, I'm not completely sure _____ is on the phone.

     (A) who   (B) whose
     (C) whom   (D) it's

_____ 2. Everyone except _____ was invited to the party.

     (A) hers   (B) she
     (C) her   (D) herself

_____ 3. If you were _____, would you allow Terri to go to the concert?

     (A) me   (B) her
     (C) my   (D) I

_____ 4. Our parents don't approve of _____ staying out past midnight.

(A) our   (B) we
(C) us   (D) ours

_____ 5. Instead of spending money on a hotel room, I think I'll stay with some friends of _____ when I go to visit Lima.

(A) me   (B) I
(C) our   (D) mine

_____ 6. The man <u>whom</u> lives above <u>my</u> apartment disturbs
                A   B
<u>me</u> with <u>his</u> extremely loud music.
C   D

_____ 7. After asking <u>it residents</u> to conserve water <u>during</u>
                    A   B
the drought, the city government <u>was</u> finally
                              C
forced to <u>shut off</u> the water for 24 hours.
           D

_____ 8. <u>Because</u> the play required several quick <u>costume</u>
         A   B
changes, the actors had to dress <u>theirselves</u> very
                           C
quickly <u>between acts</u>.
        D

_____ 9. Between <u>you and I</u>, I think Patricia is gaining
                         A

    weight <u>because</u> she has <u>little time</u> for exercise <u>with</u>
             B   C   D

    her full schedule of classes.

_____ 10. I <u>don't mind</u> sharing <u>me</u> lunch <u>with you</u>, but <u>I only</u>
              A   B   C   D

    brought peanut butter crackers.

Lets finish the **PFR** section by examining errors in **pronoun reference**. You might call this the *logical* use of pronouns; certain pronouns are used to refer to certain types of nouns and should be used correctly to avoid illogical reference.

कुछ निश्चित सर्वनामों का उपयोग कुछ निश्चित प्रकार की संज्ञा को व्यक्त करने के लिए किया जाता है । असंगत हवाले से बचने के लिए इनका उपयोग सावधानी से करना चाहिये ।

Obviously, you do not want to use *he* if referring to a girl or *they* if referring to an apple. But some other reference errors may not be so obviously incorrect.

You can use **that** or **whose** for all types of nouns. But use **which** for only things, collective nouns, and animals (in general). **Who** and **whom** can be used only with people and pets.

Notice the distinction between animals in general and pets. The way we refer to an animal depends upon our relationship with that particular animal. If it is a pet, if you know the animal's name, you can refer to it like a person. The dog walking down the street that you don't know personally is an **it**, while your dog at home named Snoopy is **he**.

EXERCISE SWE-37

Directions: Examine the pronoun reference in the following sentences. If the sentences are correct, write **OK** in the blank. If they are incorrect, put an (**X**).

__X__ 1. The river who separates the U.S. and Mexico is called the Rio Grande.

_____ 2. The dentist that I go to is from Japan.

_____ 3. The arrival who was expected at noon will be half an hour late.

_____ 4. The musician whom I hired is a classical violinist.

_____ 5. The newspaper that he writes for is published in English.

_____ 6. Has anyone seen the stack of papers which I left on my desk?

_____ 7. The professor that teaches my class is a very nice person.

_____ 8. The surgeon which performed the operation is quite young.

_____ 9. The artist who painted this picture is well known.

_____ 10. The furniture who the couple selected was on sale.

_____ 11. The books which I found on the subject are extremely useful.

_____ 12. Animals that work in the circus are often mistreated.

_____ 13. I think it was our dog who dug up the roses.

_____ 14. The mother whose son won the race must be very proud.

_____ 15. The computer who I want to buy is quite expensive.

Just one more note about pronoun reference. Pronouns which begin adjective clauses (such as *who, which, that*) should refer only to nouns or pronouns. Normally, they will immediately follow the noun or pronoun and should not follow verbs, adjectives, or other parts of speech.

सर्वनाम जो विशेषण खंड (जैसे कि कौन , जो , वो) से शुरू होते हैं केवल संज्ञा और सर्वनाम से संबंधित होते चाहिए । साधारणतया वो संज्ञा और सर्वनाम के बाद में आते है , वे क्रिया , विशेषण और वाक्य के अन्य भागों के बाद में नहीं आते।

Notice the correct and incorrect reference in the following sentences:

wrong: The weather was <u>rainy which</u> made the football field muddy.

right: It was the rainy weather which made the football field muddy.

wrong: The test was <u>difficult which</u> the students were not prepared for.

right: The students were not prepared for the difficult test.

POP QUIZ

Can you translate these words into English?

"सूखा", "बाढ़"

Which word is a countable noun and which one is a non-countable noun?

Try to correct the following pronoun errors and explain why they are wrong:

If you were me...Between you and I...

5-Step
TOEFL Prep
for Hindi Speakers

QUICK CHECK
Grammar Problem Areas

STEP ONE

| MC | Main Clause |
| SC | Subordinate Clause |

STEP TWO

S=V	Subject-Verb Agreement
S=P	Subject-Pronoun Agreement
VTF	Verb Tense or Form
PFR	Pronoun Form or Reference

STEP THREE

| > VBL | Verbals |
| WF | Word Form |

STEP FOUR

WO	Word Order
PS	Parallel Structure
UR	Unnecessary Repetition

STEP FIVE

| CU | Correct Usage |

Verbals

Gerund & Infinitive Subjects

Active & Passive Verbal Adjectives

Verbal Phrases

EXERCISE SWE-38

Directions: Using the abbreviations that identify each type of error, classify the following ten errors, then try to correct the errors. Only ten of the twelve types of errors are listed.

CU   1.   An university degree is required of all the teaching assistants.

S=P   2.   One of my five brothers will complete their college degree this year.

WF   3.   It is extremely danger to use electrical appliances near water.

MC   4.   The Room it was painted by Van Gogh, who is considered to be one of the most important impressionist artists.

WO   5.   Only after completing her degree in comparative linguistics Mary began studying Japanese.

SC   6.   Although it is strong, aluminum has many industrial uses.

VTF   7.   The test had already began when Jamie arrived.

PFR   8.   Although he is hardly ever used by many people, the metric system is the official system of measurement in the United States.

VBL   9. A lack of rain and the burned sun caused the plants to slowly die.

UR   10. It is hoped that the jury will reach a just and fair decision.

We begin STEP THREE with a study of verbals. In this section (**VBL**) we will examine the use of verbals, or words that are derived from verbs but do not function as verbs. In English, any given word might function in a number of different ways within a sentence. In this section we will review the function of infinitives and gerunds (this is introduced in the **MC** section) and study verbal adjectives and verbal phrases.

In the following examples, notice how the word *playing* could be used as a gerund, a verb (with the verb *to be*), or a verbal adjective.

Playing football is good exercise. (gerund subject)

Carl **is playing** football with his friends. (verb)

The boy **playing** football is my brother. (verbal adjective)

Some students confuse infinitives and prepositional phrases that begin with *to*. Notice the difference in the following example:

prepositional phrases: to the dance, to church, to Puerto Rico

infinitives: to dance, to play, to sing

सामान्य क्रिया , एक सरल और सम्बद्ध प्रकार की क्रिया होती है जो शब्द "to"के साथ उपयोग होती है । शब्द "to" का उपयोग पुर्वसर्गिक वाक्यों को मिलाने के लिए भी किया जा सकता है ।

Exercise SWE-39

Directions: In the blanks, write **PREP** for prepositional phrases and **INF** for infinitives.

1. _INF_ to cry
2. _____ to the park
3. _____ to dance
4. _____ to park
5. _____ to benefit
6. _____ to peace
7. _____ to disqualify
8. _____ to disturb
9. _____ to happiness
10. _____ to meditate

11. _____ to sing
12. _____ to reach
13. _____ to swim
14. _____ to stand
15. _____ to pursue
16. _____ to good health
17. _____ to encounter
18. _____ to the market
19. _____ to reality
20. _____ to prosperity

Now that we can distinguish between prepositional phrases and infinitives, let's practice more with infinitives. Remember an infinitive (as well as a gerund, noun, pronoun, or noun clause) can function as the subject of a sentence.

EXERCISE SWE-40

Directions: Examine the following sentences and underline and label the subject with (**S**), the verb with (**V**), and infinitive with (**I**). In some of the sentences you will find an infinitive subject. Identify them with (**IS**).

             S   **V**   **I**

1. Children love to paint.

2. We go to school to learn.

3. To drive under the influence of alcohol is illegal.

4. Jimmy wants to drive to New York.

5. Doctors need to keep themselves updated on new medical reports.

6. She went to the bakery to buy a cake.

7. To control insects spray the garden with an insecticide.

8. Researchers hope to find a solution to the problem.

9. To eat only one meal per day is not healthy.

10. I want to see the new movie this weekend.

11. The marching band is going to perform at the football game.

12. Giovanna likes to cook lasagne and other Italian dishes.

13. We plan to put up the Christmas tree tomorrow.

14. We need to plan the party this week.

15. I hope to make a high score on my TOEFL exam.

Now we'll do the same thing with gerunds. Remember, a gerund does not function as a verb. It needs a verb *to be* to activate it into a verb. No verb *to be,* no verb!

सामान्य क्रिया के अंत में "ing" लगाने से इसे to the simple form of a
verb (without "to") । क्रियात्मक संज्ञा तब तक क्रिया की तरह काम
नहीं करती जब तक उसे क्रिया "to be" के साथ सक्रिय न किया जाए ।

EXERCISE SWE-41

Directions: Examine the following sentences and underline
and label the subject with **(S)**, the verb with **(V)**, and the ger-
und with **(G)**. In some of the sentences you will find a gerund
subject. Identify these with **(GS)**. In some of the sentences
there is no gerund.

        GS   **V**
1.   <u>Smoking</u> <u>causes</u> cancer.

2.   My grandmother is arriving this afternoon.

3.   They enjoy playing soccer on Sundays.

4.   Backpacking in mountainous regions requires special
equipment.

5.   The orchestra is practicing a Vivaldi concerto.

6.   Learning a new language is both difficult and fun.

7.   He is becoming skilful at playing tennis.

8.   Flooding was caused by the breaking of the dam.

9.   Mailing early insures delivery before the holidays.

10.   The players are obviously becoming tired.

11.   She thanked me for babysitting her children.

12.   Swimming is a very complete exercise.

13.   The family is going on vacation next week.

14.   Rollerblading without knee pads is risky.

15.   Greg Louganis perfected the art of diving.

Before we complete the **VBL** section with a study of verbal adjectives and verbal adjective phrases, let's do a **Mini TOEFL** practice exercise.

MINI TOEFL-12

Directions: In questions 1-5, choose the one word or phrase that best completes the sentence. In questions 6-10, identify the underlined word(s) that should be changed to make the sentence correct. **Time: 6 minutes**

_____ 1. The students _____ working on their exams for nearly two hours.

(A) which are   (B) is
(C) have been   (D) who have been

_____ 2. Many retirees move to Florida _____.

(A) for to live   (B) to live
(C) for living   (D) living

_____ 3. We enjoy _____ in the ocean more than in a pool.

(A) to swim   (B) are swimming
(C) swim   (D) swimming

_____ 4. Your backhand _____ day by day.

(A) is improving   (B) improving
(C) are improving   (D) to improve

Note that after the verb _enjoy_ a gerund is used. Other verbs require only gerunds. Refer to Appendix C at the end of the book.

_____ 5. The students _____ to complete their final projects before Friday.

(A) is trying   (B) has been trying
(C) trying   (D) are trying

_____ 6. <u>Painting it</u> is one of <u>many ways</u> <u>to express</u> <u>oneself</u>
       A   B   C   D
artistically.

_____ 7. <u>Donating money</u> to the orphanage <u>one</u> of the
          A   B
<u>kindest</u> things the rich man <u>ever did</u>.
   C   D

_____ 8. <u>Nearly all</u> of my classmates <u>have been studying</u>
       A   B
English <u>since</u> more <u>than</u> five years.
       C   D

_____ 9. <u>Studying</u> Hindi <u>is probably</u> one of the most
     A   B
<u>difficult thing</u> I have <u>ever done</u>.
    C   D

_____ 10. The kids <u>to sleep</u> <u>early last</u> night <u>because</u> they had
          A   B   C
to <u>wake up</u> very early in the morning.
    D

Every verb in English has two **verbal adjective** forms. They function like ordinary adjectives, but they are derived from verbs. A verbal adjective can be in the form of the present participle (which ends in *ing*) or the past participle (which ends in *d, t,* or *n*). For example, the verb **to eat** has two verbal adjective forms: **eating** and **eaten**. From the verb **to surprise** we have **surprising** and **surprised**.

अंग्रेजी में हर क्रिया की दो शाब्दिक विशेषण प्रकार होते हैं । वह साधारण विशेषण की भांति काम करते हैं , परन्तु उन्हें क्रिया से निकाला जाता है । शाब्दिक विशेषण वर्तमान कृदन्त (जो ing पर खत्म होते हैं) या भूत कृदन्त (जो n, d, or t पर खत्म होते हैं) के रूप में हो सकते हैं ।

EXERCISE SWE-42

Directions: Examine the following sentences. Find and put parentheses ( ) around the verbal adjectives.

1. The (burning) forest has made the people (living) around the area very nervous.

2. Of the many varieties of plants grown in hanging baskets, ferns are the most popular.

3. Football players recruited by the coach should report to practice three months before the first game.

4. The bubbling soup must be left to cool before it is served to the hungry children.

5. The film showing at the cinema was directed by an aspiring actor.

6. The music playing now on the radio reminds me of the music that was popular fifteen years ago.

7. Folding chairs were set up around the pool to accommodate the exhausted guests.

8. The girls swimming in the lake are spending their summer vacation here with their parents.

9. The accused defendant is scheduled to make a court appearance during the coming week.

10. The man selling ice cream in the park is sometimes frightened by the barking dogs.

11. The torn pillows can be easily mended by an experienced upholsterer.

12. Neglected and abused children are sometimes removed from the custody of their parents.

13. The air circulating through this building is much cleaner than the polluted air outside.

14. The rooms reserved at the hotel will be available after noon.

15. A tossed salad usually includes shredded lettuce, sliced tomatoes, grated cheese, and a dressing.

Do you think you can distinguish between verbal adjectives and active verbs? The next exercise will give you some practice.

EXERCISE SWE-43

Directions: Examine the following words. Decide if they are active verbs or verbal adjectives and write them in the appropriate column below.

is walking	eating	looking	drank
are playing	looks	will call	jumping
selling	acting	have been fed	crying
speaking	was put	remembering	are studying
were helping	participating	reviewing	is cooking

ACTIVE VERBS   **VERBAL ADJECTIVES**

As discussed, a verbal adjective can take the form of a present participle (*ing*) or a past participle (*d, n, t*). It is necessary to consider the noun that your verbal adjective is describing to choose the correct form. If the noun is actively *doing* the action, use the present participle form. If the noun is passively *receiving* the action, use the past participle form.

जैसे बताया गया, एक शाब्दिक विशेषण वर्तमान कृदन्त (ing) या भूत कृदन्त (n, d, t) की जगह ले सकता है । इसलिए सही चुनाव के लिए उस संज्ञा पर गौर करना जरुरी है जिसे आपका शाब्दिक विशेषण वर्णित कर रहा है । अगर आपकी संज्ञा सक्रिय रूप में कोई काम कर रही है तो वर्तमान कृदन्त का उपयोग करें लेकिन अगर संज्ञा निष्क्रिय रूप में काम कर रही हो तो भूत कृदन्त का उपयोग करें ।

Examine the following examples:

The **excited** children. The **exciting** movie. If you have confusion, think of the following illustration, which should make it clear.

Using the verb **to threaten,** "धमकी देना" , notice that the snake is actively **threatening,** while the mouse is passively **threatened.**

ING   ED

Let's practice forming active and passive verbal adjectives.

EXERCISE SWE-44

Directions: In this exercise, you'll be given a verb and two nouns. Using the (1) verb, describe the (2) first noun actively and the (3) second noun passively.

1.   (1) to burn (2) sun (3) dinner

        _____burning sun_____   _____burned dinner_____

2.   (1) to convince (2) argument (3) students

        _____   _____

3.   (1) to surprise (2) present (3) child

        _____   _____

4.   (1) to annoy (2) noise (3) parents

        _____   _____

5.   (1) to exhaust (2) exam (3) test takers

        _____   _____

6.   (1) to entertain (2) actors (3) audience

        _____   _____

7.   (1) to frighten (2) story (3) kids

_____   _____

8.   (1) to amuse (2) joke (3) guests

_____   _____

9.   (1) to entertain (2) clowns (3) public

_____   _____

10.   (1) to excite (2) soccer match (3) fans

_____   _____

Now let's get a little closer to the TOEFL format. In the following exercise you'll be given a choice of two verbal adjectives. Try to find the incorrect one.

EXERCISE SWE-45

Directions: In the following sentences there are two underlined verbal adjectives. Try to find the incorrect one and write the corresponding letter (A or B) in the blank.

___A___ 1. The <u>boring</u> students nearly fell asleep during the
                 A
              <u>boring</u> class.
                 B

_____ 2. The <u>excited</u> movie was enjoyed by the <u>excited</u>
                 A   B
              children.

_____ 3. The <u>required</u> reading is found in that book
                 A
              <u>advertising</u> by the bookstore.
                 B

_____ 4. The <u>thought-provoked</u> question was examined by
                 A
              the <u>interested</u> lawyer.
                    B

_____ 5. An <u>experienced</u> technician needs to examine the
                 A
              <u>malfunctioned</u> computer.
                 B

_____ 6. Margaret and her friends were <u>amazed</u> by the
                                            A

        <u>astounded</u> magician.
        B

_____ 7. The freshly <u>painting</u> wall makes the <u>unpainted</u>
                      A   B

        wall look drab.

_____ 8. The artist <u>contracting</u> to paint the portrait is known
                        A

        for his <u>inspired</u> works of art.
                B

_____ 9. A penny <u>saved</u> is a penny <u>earning</u>.
                  A   B

_____ 10. The <u>freezing</u> weather killed the flowers <u>planting</u>
                A   B

        by the mailbox.

For just a little more practice with verbal adjectives, before we move on to verbal phrases, let's do another short exercise.

EXERCISE SWE-46

Directions: Notice the verbal adjectives in the following sentences. If the sentences are correct, write **OK** in the blank. If they are incorrect, put an (**X**).

__X__ 1. Steamed broccoli is much healthier than boiling broccoli.

_____ 2. The speeding car was eventually stopped by the pursued police.

_____ 3. Crying children should be taken to the nursery located on the first floor.

_____ 4. The TOEFL exam is now administered in a computerizing format.

_____ 5. Your thesis topics must be approved by your counselor if they are not among the specifically assigned topics listed in this memorandum.

_____ 6. The struggling student found the course material too advancing.

_____ 7. The new Volkswagen Beetle is produced in Mexico and exported to the United States.

_____ 8. The uniformed guard kept a close eye on the suspecting shoplifter.

_____ 9. The lost puppy wondered around the neighborhood for hours before its worried owner finally found him playing near the woods.

_____ 10. Concerned students should be present at the council meeting to voice their opinions on related issues.

When analyzing TOEFL questions, it is usually best to **eliminate phrases** from your consideration. They usually have nothing to do with the error but complicate the sentence and make it confusing. By "throwing away" the phrases, it's easier to find the error.

However, we must be careful with one particular type of phrase. It's called a **verbal phrase** and could very well cause an error. Follow this rule: when you begin a sentence with a verbal phrase, make sure you have logical agreement with the subject of the main clause that follows. For example, it would be incorrect to say: **After** _finishing_ **lunch, the** _football game_ **started.** We don't have logical agreement between the verbal _finishing_ and the subject _football game_. It's not logical because a football game can't finish lunch!

> मौखिक वाक्यांशों की वाक्य के प्रधान उपवाक्य के उद्देश से न्यायसंगत समानता होनी चाहिए ।

Correcting sentences like this one is a little more complicated than simply changing a word or two. You can do one of two things to correct it.

(1)   Change the verbal phrase to a subordinate clause. For example: *After we finished lunch,* the football game started.

(2)   Change the subject of the main clause so that it agrees with the verbal phrase. For example: After finishing lunch, *we* watched the football game.

When you're taking the TOEFL exam and you find a sentence that begins with a verbal phrase, check to be sure that there is logical agreement with the subject of the main clause. Of course, the difficulty here might be recognizing the verbal phrase. The following exercise should help you recognize verbal phrases. We will practice reducing subordinate clauses to verbal phrases just to have some practice in forming, and, hopefully, recognizing them.

All of the sentences in the following exercise are correct. And all of the subordinate clauses can be reduced to verbal phrases while maintaining logical agreement between the phrase and the subject of the main clause. One tip: when reducing subordinate clauses to verbal phrases, keep the introductory time words, but omit the introductory cause words.

Examine the following examples:

Subordinate Clause: While he was cooking dinner, the chef burned his hand.

Verbal Phrase: While cooking dinner, the chef burned his hand.

Subordinate Clause: Because she is sick, the girl didn't go to school.

Verbal Phrase: Being sick, the girl didn't go to school.

EXERCISE SWE-47

Directions: Rewrite the following sentences. Change the subordinate clauses to verbal phrases.

1. While he was driving to work, the man listened to the radio.

    <u>While driving to work, the man listened to the radio.</u>

2. Because he had won the election, the politician gave a press conference.

    _____

    _____

3. After he ran all the way home, the little boy was exhausted.

    _____

    _____

4. Because it has a high caffeine content, coffee is avoided by insomniacs.

    _____

    _____

5. After he had graduated from college, Mike was offered a good job.

    _____

    _____

6. Because they require little water, cacti grow well in the desert.

    _____

    _____

7. Because it is easy to grow, tomatoes are a popular back yard vegetable.

    _____

    _____

8. After it had been checked, the computer's phone modem functioned perfectly.

    _____

    _____

9. When it is consumed frequently in large amounts, alcohol can cause liver problems.

    _____

    _____

10.   Since they are high in calories, regular soft drinks are
        often substituted with diet soft drinks.

        _____

        _____

Now you should be able to recognize verbal phrases. Again,
when taking the TOEFL, if your sentence begins with a verbal
phrase, check the subject of the main clause that follows to
make sure you have logical agreement. Let's conclude our
study of verbal phrases with the following exercise. All of the
sentences begin with verbal phrases, so check the subject of
the main clause.

EXERCISE SWE-48

Directions: Underline the verbal in the verbal phrase and the
subject of the main clause. Write **OK** if the sentence is correct
and an (**X**) if it is wrong.

    __X__   1. Hoping to generate more education funds, a lottery
                might be approved by the legislature.

    _____ 2. When applying for admission to an American
                university, the TOEFL exam is often required of
                students.

    _____ 3. While cleaning the house, the maid listened to the
                radio.

_____ 4. After eating too much candy, a stomachache caused discomfort to the little boy.

_____ 5. Standing in a long line, the sun burned the faces of the movie goers.

_____ 6. Made of fresh berries, the piping hot pie smelled delicious.

_____ 7. Arriving to her office late, Christine missed the important staff meeting.

_____ 8. Running quickly around the track, his blood pressure began to rise.

_____ 9. Living in Los Angeles, the couple was accustomed to heavy traffic.

_____ 10. Loving the opera, the performance of *Carmen* was a treat for Alex.

_____ 11. Considering herself to be homely, parties were rarely attended by Jennifer.

_____ 12. Considered by many to be the greatest author of all time, the works of Charles Dickens are still enjoyed by many readers.

_____ 13. Offering discounts of up to 25%, the store recorded record sales.

_____ 14. Located in the southwest U.S., Texas has a very hot climate.

_____ 15. Powered by batteries, electric cars do not pollute the air.

_____ 16. After practicing hard for several hours every day, the difficult routine was perfected by the young gymnast.

_____ 17. After being carried for several hours in the hot sun with no water, the beautiful arrangement of flowers began to wilt.

_____ 18. After working all day on his computer, Mickey's eyes were very tired.

_____ 19. When plugging in the TV with wet hands, an electrical shock was felt by the repairman.

_____ 20. Having already spent too much money using her credit cards, the shopper decided it was time to leave the mall.

That concludes our study of verbals. Before we continue with the word form (**WF**) section, let's do a Mini TOEFL practice exercise.

 Here's a verb you might not know. _Wilt_ means "शिथिल होना".

MINI TOEFL-13

Directions: In questions 1-5, choose the one word or phrase that best completes the sentence. In questions 6-10, identify the underlined word(s) that should be changed to make the sentence correct. **Time: 6 minutes**

_____ 1. _____ only one hundred dollars, the couple was able to save several thousand in two years.

    (A) Began with   (B) Beginning with
    (C) Had begun with   (D) To begin with

_____ 2. Though known more for amusement parks and movies, _____.

    (A) Broadway musicals have recently been produced by the Walt Disney Company.

    (B) produced recently by the Walt Disney Company have been Broadway musicals.

    (C) there have been Broadway musicals produced recently by the Walt Disney Company.

    (D) the Walt Disney Company has recently produced Broadway musicals.

_____ 3. _____ by the researcher's report, the students asked many questions.

(A) Stimulated   (B) Stimulating
(C) Were stimulated   (D)They were stimulated

_____ 4. Having performed in public only once, _____ about giving the recital.

(A) the violinist she was nervous

(B) the violinist was nervous

(C) nervousness was felt by the violinist

(D) felt nervous the violinist

_____ 5. _____ in a tiny town all her life, Irma was unaccustomed to the traffic and contamination of a big city.

(A) Lived   (B) Having lived
(C) Had lived   (D) She lived

_____ 6. Located <u>between</u> Birmingham and Mobile,
                        A
<u>the history of</u> the city <u>of</u> Montgomery, Alabama <u>is</u>
          B   C   D
interesting.

_____ 7. While skiing down the <u>steep mountain</u> in <u>freezing</u>
                                              A   B

weather <u>the nose of</u> the skier became very cold
            C

and decided <u>to stop for a rest</u>.
                    D

_____ 8. <u>After looked</u> all day for the perfect, new furniture,
           A

<u>the couple</u> still <u>could</u> not find exactly what they
      B   C

were looking <u>for</u>.
            D

_____ 9. After finishing dinner, the <u>doorbell chimed and</u>
                               A

doctor went <u>to see</u> who <u>was</u> at the door <u>at such a</u>
           B   C   D

late hour.

_____ 10. <u>Flied through</u> the air with the <u>greatest of ease</u>, the
        A   B

trapeze <u>artist</u> suddenly fell <u>from the air</u> onto the
        C   D

safety net below.

5-Step
TOEFL Prep
for Hindi Speakers

QUICK CHECK
Grammar Problem Areas

STEP ONE

MC	Main Clause
SC	Subordinate Clause

STEP TWO

S=V	Subject-Verb Agreement
S=P	Subject-Pronoun Agreement
VTF	Verb Tense or Form
PFR	Pronoun Form or Reference

STEP THREE

VBL	Verbals
> WF	Word Form

STEP FOUR

WO	Word Order
PS	Parallel Structure
UR	Unnecessary Repetition

STEP FIVE

CU	Correct Usage

Word Form

Suffixes & Derived Forms

Incorrect Gerunds

"LY" Adverbs & Adjectives

Adjective-verb Combinations,
Sense Verbs, Linking Verbs

Comparative/Superlative Forms

EXERCISE SWE-49

Directions: Using the abbreviations that identify each type of error, classify the following ten errors, then try to correct the errors. Only ten of the twelve types of errors are listed.

SC   1. Insect repellents are available in sprays or lotions provide an effective solution to the mosquito problem.

PFR   2. The stories whom appeared in the book were accompanied by beautiful illustrations.

S=V   3. The elephant, along with most of the other animals in the circus, are poorly cared for.

WO   4. I love having lunch with Tania because she always has funny something to tell.

S=P   5. The teacher along with all of the kindergarten children is eating their lunch.

VBL   6. While looking at the garden through the window, it started to rain.

MC   7. The church group back yesterday from its trip to Europe.

PS   8. The art teacher asked the students to paint their pictures slowly, carefully, and using a lot of imagination.

WF   9.   Emotion problems can cause a variety of other problems, such as depression, alcoholism, and paranoia.

UR   10.   During the sale, the department store reduced its prices up to 50% less.

We finish STEP THREE with a study of word from (**WF**). In this section, we will see that sometimes a sentence on the TOEFL exam might have a word that is not exactly the wrong word, but is not in the correct form. For example, perhaps we have a noun that should be in the adjective form. Refer to number nine in the above exercise. Notice that *emotion* should be *emotional*. We need the adjective form, not the noun form, to describe the noun *problem*.

Examine the following sentences. This should give you a good idea of what is meant by **WF** errors.

Cynthia wants to study *chemical*. (chemistry)

It is *danger* to ride a motorcycle without a helmet. (dangerous)

The teacher might not accept my paper with this ugly *erasing*. (erasure)

Erasure is a rather unusual word that you'll probably not use too often. In Hindi it means "मिटाना" . And what exactly is an erasure? In the box below, scribble for a couple of seconds with a pencil. Now lightly erase it. The mark that is left behind is an erasure!

It might help you to remember this word by thinking about the famous British pop group. Can you think of a song that this band made famous?

I don't feel *well* today. I have a headache. (good)

In my opinion, Mary is the *most pretty* girl in the world. (prettiest)

In this section, we'll study derived words—words which are formed from other words—and their relationships (how a noun is formed from a verb, an adverb from an adjective, etc.) Knowing how a word functions is a very important skill—especially for the TOEFL exam. Maybe you won't always know exactly what the word means, but it will help to at least know how its grammatical function.

Be familiar with the following suffixes that can be added to verbs to make derived nouns: **y, al, ure, ence, ance, ment, ation, sion**. When a word ends in one of these suffixes, you should recognize it as a noun, *even if you have no idea what the word means!* Studying these suffixes will also help you later when we examine gerunds vs. derived nouns.

> यह संज्ञा बनाने के लिए सामान्यतया प्रयोग होने वाले प्रत्यय है जो क्रिया से उत्पन्न होते है ।

EXERCISE SWE-50

Directions: Using the previously listed suffixes, try to form derived nouns using the following verbs. Write the derived nouns in the spaces.

1.	fail	_failure_	11. refuse	_____
2.	deliver	_____	12. advertise	_____
3.	try	_____	13. observe	_____
4.	withdraw	_____	14. judge	_____
5.	accept	_____	15. exist	_____
6.	move	_____	16. press	_____
7.	examine	_____	17. recover	_____
8.	discover	_____	18. correspond	_____
9.	please	_____	19. form	_____
10.	erase	_____	20. oblige	_____

Withdrawal means "नकद निकालना". The next time you go to an ATM (automated teller machine), you might notice this word if there are English instructions.

EXERCISE SWE-51

Directions: Examine the following sentences and try to find the nouns that are derived from verbs. Underline them and write in the blanks the verbs from which they were derived.

propose 1. Your book <u>proposal</u> will be reviewed by our chief editor.

_____ 2. Flattery will get you nowhere.

_____ 3. Do you believe in the existence of ghosts?

_____ 4. His mastery of the violin represents many years of study.

_____ 5. You should try a classified advertisement to sell your car.

_____ 6. We need more help with the decorations for the prom.

_____ 7. Don't jump to conclusions without examining the facts.

_____ 8. The cat's refusal to eat is a sure sign of sickness.

_____ 9. Please forward all correspondence to my attention.

_____ 10. Although the death penalty is highly controversial, executions still occur in the U.S.

_____ 11. Fortunately, we have a great deal of coherence among our staff.

_____ 12. Books provide one of life's simple pleasures.

_____ 13. The man was charged with concealment of a weapon.

_____ 14. All personnel are required to take a medical examination.

_____ 15. Thank you for your thoughtful words of encouragement.

It is also sometimes possible to use a gerund as a derived noun. However, this type of derived noun can only be used if no other noun form exists. In other words, in formal English, you shouldn't use *preferring* as a noun because *preference* exists.

> क्रियावाचक संज्ञा को संज्ञा के स्थान पर तभी प्रयोग करना चाहिए जब वाक्य में संज्ञा न हो ।

This little situation can cause some problems. How do you know if a verb has a derived form or if the use of the gerund form is permissible? Unfortunately, there are no rules that can be applied—there is no way to look at a verb and know if it has a derived form or not. This is simply a matter of practice and experience—of vocabulary skill. The best method of improving this skill is to be as familiar as possible with the common suffixes (listed previously) that are used to formulate a derived noun from a verb.

We'll continue with a couple of exercises designed to give you practice with this.

EXERCISE SWE-52

Directions: Examine the gerunds. If the gerund can be used as a noun write (**OK**) in the blank. But if another derived noun form exists, write the correct form in the blank. Remember: you can only use gerunds if another derived form does *not* exist.

agreement	1. agreeing	_____	11. exciting
_____	2. deciding	_____	12. leaving
_____	3. preferring	_____	13. existing
_____	4. resigning	_____	14. implying
_____	5. refusing	_____	15. transforming
_____	6. learning	_____	16. dividing
_____	7. recovering	_____	17. pressing
_____	8. abandoning	_____	18. automating
_____	9. installing	_____	19. departing
_____	10. erasing	_____	20. arranging

EXERCISE SWE-53

Directions: The following sentences contain at least one gerund. If all gerunds are used correctly write (**OK**) in the blank. But if one is incorrect, underline it and write the derived noun that should be used instead in the blank.

departure 1. The <u>departing</u> of flight 2356 is scheduled for 4:00 PM.

_____ 2. New linguistic studies show that learning a language is not easier for children than adults, as many had thought.

_____ 3. The resigning of the college president came as a shock to the faculty and students.

_____ 4. The couple went to months of counseling before they agreed on a separation.

_____ 5. Your failing to improve your test score might suggest you need to prepare more.

_____ 6. The arranging of books in our library is consistent with the guidelines of the Dewey Decimal system.

_____ 7. The developing of a new curriculum is one of the most challenging aspects of the teacher's job.

_____ 8. Please go to the front desk for informing on local tourist sites.

_____ 9. Although actually illegal, jaywalking is ignored by police in most cities.

_____ 10. On the Listening Comprehension section of the TOEFL, you must pay attention not only to the meaning but also to the implying of the words you hear.

_____ 11. You must be careful when making cash withdrawing in large cities as many people are robbed everyday at ATMs.

_____ 12. Check your pronouns and verbs for correct agreeing with the subject.

_____ 13. Alexander Bell had originally been credited with the discovering of the telephone.

_____ 14. The majority of the world's population believes in the existing of some higher being or god.

_____ 15. Perhaps because of his urban upbringing, Mark found life in the rural town boring.

And that brings us to our next **Mini TOEFL** practice exercise.

Mini TOEFL-14

Directions: In questions 1-5, choose the one word or phrase that best completes the sentence. In questions 6-10, identify the underlined word(s) that should be changed to make the sentence correct. **Time: 6 minutes**

_____ 1. The _____ in the banquet hall should accommo-date 500 people.

(A) seat arranging   (B) arranging of seats
(C) seating arranging (D) arrangement of seats

_____ 2. The rapid _____ is changing the face of our city.

(A) developing of new neighborhoods
(B) development of new neighborhoods
(C) neighborhood's new developing
(D) neighboring developing

_____ 3. The _____ has not been met with unanimous sup-port.

(A) president's recommendation
(B) recommending of the president
(C) president's recommending
(D) presidential recommending

_____ 4. _____ is a highly controversial issue on the United States.

(A) Desegregating of schools
(B) School desegregation
(C) School desegregating
(D) Scholarly desegregating

_____ 5. _____ it started to rain.

    (A) While finishing dinner
    (B) Having finished dinner
    (C) After we finished dinner
    (D) After finishing dinner

_____ 6. The <u>company's</u> <u>expanding into</u> Latin American
              A   B
    <u>countries is</u> responsible for a 25% increase <u>in</u>
         C   D
    gross revenue.

_____ 7. <u>Severe bleeding</u> can be <u>controlled for</u> applying
         A   B
    <u>pressure</u> to the injury for <u>several minutes</u>.
      C   D

_____ 8. It's not <u>so much</u> what you said that <u>bothers me</u> as
            A   B
    the <u>implying</u> hidden <u>between the lines</u> of your let-
         C   D
    ter.

_____ 9. The <u>departing of</u> the next <u>flight to</u> France <u>will be</u>
         A   B   C
    delayed until tomorrow <u>due to</u> severe weather in
                       D
    the Paris area.

_____ 10. Many are becoming <u>disgruntled</u> with the <u>failing of</u>
                                       A   B
the U.S. Congress <u>to pass</u> legislation that reduces
                         C
taxes for <u>the</u> working class.
              D

We continue with our study of **WF** with more suffixes. Remember, knowing how a word functions, even when you don't know what the word means, is an important skill that will be very useful when taking the TOEFL exam. We're now going to see suffixes that indicate that a word is a noun that refers to people and suffixes that indicate that a word is an adjective.

The following are examples of some common suffixes that refer to people: **ist, er, ian, ant, ster, tor, ic, ite, eer, ee**. As you can see, there are quite a few.

EXERCISE SWE-54

Directions: Using the list of abstract nouns (nouns which refer to intangible things) try to form nouns that refer to people. Use the suffixes listed previously (try to use each one only once) and write the nouns referring to people by the abstract form.

1. employment   _employee_   6. youth   _____

2. alcoholism   _____   7. service   _____

3. invention   _____   8. carpentry   _____

4. sociability   _____   9. racket   _____

5. magic   _____   10. biology   _____

Some of the suffixes that are used to derive an adjective from a noun include: **ful**, **esque**, **en**, **an**, **some**, **ish**, **ic**, **able**, **less**, **al**, **ly**, **ary**, **ive**, **ous**, **proof**, **ory**, and **y**.

EXERCIE SWE-55

Directions: Try to form adjectives using the following list of nouns. Use the suffixes listed previously to help you.

1. peace _____peaceful_____   9. impression _____

2. penny _____   10. picture _____

3. gold _____   11. fanatic _____

4. Nebraska _____   12. ghost _____

5. introduction _____   13. awe _____

6. self _____   14. action _____

7. fire _____   15. glamour _____

8. majesty _____   16. chill _____

It's a good idea to study the derived words in the two previous exercises—**pay attention to the suffixes**. They should help you recognize nouns that refer to people and adjectives—even when the word is not familiar to you. For a little extra practice, try forming sentences using the derived words.

Next, we'll learn to distinguish between adjectives and adverbs that end in *ly*. It's always important to know in what form a word is functioning, but this could be particularly important here in identifying errors in parallel structure. Imagine that you have a sentence with what appears to be several *ly* adjectives separated by commas. It seems the parallel structure is OK. But one of the words you assumed to be an *ly* adjective is really an *ly* adverb. So the parallel structure is not good.

It's easy to tell the difference between an *ly* adjective and an *ly* adverb. Just take away the *ly* and examine the base word that is left. If you are left with a noun, you have an *ly* adjective. If you are left with an adjective, you have an *ly* adverb.

"ly" प्रत्यय को संज्ञा के साथ जोड़ कर विशेषण बनाया जाता है या विशेषण के साथ जोड़ कर एक क्रिया-विशेषण ।

This process is illustrated in the box below. For example, *cost-ly* is an adjective because *cost* is a noun, while *beautifully* is an adverb because *beautiful* is an adjective.

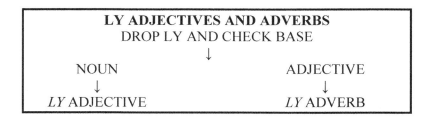

LY ADJECTIVES AND ADVERBS
DROP LY AND CHECK BASE
↓
NOUN   ADJECTIVE
↓   ↓
LY ADJECTIVE   *LY* ADVERB

Try the following exercise for practice with this.

EXERCISE SWE-56

Directions: Indicate if the following words are adjectives or adverbs by writing (**ADJ**) or (**ADV**)in the blanks.

1. seriously	_ADV_	11. beautifully	_____
2. shapely	_____	12. imaginatively	_____
3. neighborly	_____	13. friendly	_____
4. patiently	_____	14. miraculously	_____
5. amazingly	_____	15. stately	_____
6. foolishly	_____	16. worldly	_____
7. elegantly	_____	17. amusingly	_____
8. monthly	_____	18. candidly	_____
9. sincerely	_____	19. costly	_____
10. perfectly	_____	20. legally	_____

Studying the relationship between word forms can be helpful. Knowing one form might help you figure out another form. Try to fill in the blanks in the following chart. After it is completed, study the relationship among the various forms. Note: you might find more than one possible option for some forms.

EXERCISE SWE-57

NOUN	VERB	ADJECTIVE	ADVERB
1. excellence			
2.		satisfactory	
3.			confidentially
4.	succeed		
5. decision			
6.		energetic	
7.			excessively
8.	repeat		
9. category			
10.		imaginative	

Now we'll practice identifying word form errors in the context of the TOEFL exam with the following Mini TOEFL practice exercise.

MINI TOEFL-15

Directions: In questions 1-5, choose the one word or phrase that best completes the sentence. In questions 6-10, identify the underlined word(s) that should be changed to make the sentence correct. **TIME: 6 minutes**

_____ 1. I hope to take several courses in _____ before finishing my degree.

    (A) comparison linguistics
    (B) comparative linguistics
    (C) comparatively linguistics
    (D) linguistic comparative

_____ 2. Water, perhaps our most important _____, is often wasted and polluted.

    (A) naturally resource
    (B) resourceful of nature
    (C) naturally resourceful
    (D) natural resource

_____ 3. To operate a small business that is a _____, a person must be willing to work extremely long hours.

    (A) success   (B) successfully
    (C) successful   (D) succeeding

_____ 4. Mark and Bill _____ planned their three days in New York City to include a Broadway show, lunch in Chinatown, and a Mets game.

(A) careful (B) care
(C) carefully (D) had a carefully

_____ 5. The small town of Canoe, Alabama _____ the Indians who once lived there.

(A) got its name from (B) its name got from
(C) got it's name from (D) it got the name from

_____ 6. Because our focus is on <u>creative writing</u>, <u>higher</u>
                                     A   B
grades will be given to those students <u>who write</u>
                                                          C
the <u>most imagination</u> essays.
          D

_____ 7. The flight attendant's <u>decision action</u> helped <u>keep</u>
                                       A   B
the situation under control <u>when</u> the airplane was
                                      C
flying through <u>turbulent weather</u>.
                      D

_____ 8. <u>The chemicals</u> plant <u>has been</u> accused of dumping
               A   B
<u>toxic wastes</u> and could be forced to pay penalties
       C
<u>that reach</u> millions of dollars.
      D

_____ 9. The head of the <u>English departmental</u> <u>is planning</u>
                                   A   B

to include TOEFL preparation courses <u>as part of</u>
                                                      C

the <u>newly developed</u> curriculum.
          D

_____ 10. Last month a Boston <u>research laboratory</u>
                                   A

<u>developers</u> a new medication that <u>might be used</u> in
    B   C

the treatment of <u>baldness in men</u>.
                    D

Most of the time adjectives are used to modify nouns and adverbs are used to modify verbs. But sometimes it is necessary to use an adjective to modify a verb—when that verb falls under one of three categories: 1) adjective-verb combinations, 2) sense verbs, 3) linking verbs.

You should not have much difficulty with the first category of verbs the 1) **adjective-verb combination** includes verbs such as: *keep quiet, open wide, break loose, stand still,* etc. Notice that the adjective becomes part of the verb.

2)   **Sense verbs** include words such as: *smell, taste, look, feel,* etc. Just make sure the verb is actually acting as a sense verb and not an action verb, in which case the normal adverb would be used. For example: The soup **smells** *good.* With my cold I can't **smell** *well.* In the first sentence *to smell* functions as a sense verb so an adjective is used to modify it. In the second sentence *to smell* functions as an action verb so an adverb is used to modify it. This is also logical. **Soup can't smell *well* because soup doesn't have a nose!**

Try to imagine a bowl of soup…

…with a nose!

3)   **Linking verbs** are similar to sense verbs. A linking verb connects the subject of a sentence to a compliment. This compliment could be an adjective which describes the subject it refers to. For example: *Phillip **is** nice.* The verb *to be* functions as a linking verb. Other linking verbs include: *appear, become, grow, get, remain, prove,* and *turn.*

Linking verbs might describe a transformation in attitude, appearance, emotional state, etc. You can usually substitute the verb *to become* without changing the meaning. Some verbs have active and linking verb meanings. If they function as an active verb, the adverb, not the adjective, is used to modify it. For example: The tree **grew** *quickly*. Tania **grew** *angry*. In the first sentence *to grow* functions as an action verb so an adverb is used to modify it. In the second sentence *to grow* functions as a linking verb so an adjective is used to modify it.

क्रिया –विशेषण को क्रिया के साथ उपयोग किया जाता है ,जब तक क्रिया निम्नलिखित तीन श्रेणियों में से एक न हो – विशेषण – क्रिया संयोग , भावनात्मक क्रिया , मिलानत्मक क्रिया । इस प्रकार की क्रिया को विशेषण द्वारा संशोधित किया जाता है ।

EXERCISE SWE-58

Directions: Examine the verbs in the following sentences and circle the correct adverb or adjective forms. Choose the adjective only if the verb falls into one of the three categories mentioned.

1. George felt (sleepy, sleepily) after driving all night.

2. The crowd got (quiet, quietly) when the curtain went up.

3.   The coach screamed (angry, angrily) at the basketball players.

4.   A few days at the beach sounds (wonderful, wonderfully).

5.   The lady looked (careful, carefully) in her desk for her wallet.

6.   Please keep (quiet, quietly) while we're in the library.

7.   When she heard the news, Jane turned (pale, palely).

8.   We felt (sad, sadly) after seeing the movie.

9.   The barbecued chicken smells really (good, well).

10.   The kids go (crazy, crazily) when they're stuck inside on rainy days.

11.   She slipped the hot soup very (careful, carefully).

12.   The dentist asked the patient to open (wide, widely).

13.   I trusted the woman because she looked (honest, honestly).

14.   The sun was shining (bright, brightly) when the picnic began.

15.   Tom grew (angry, angrily) when he heard the news.

16.   The students were almost asleep when the bell (final, finally) sounded.

17. After two weeks without a bath, the dog didn't smell (good, well).

18. The audience laughed (uncontrollable, uncontrollably) at the comedian.

19. The bouquet of flowers smells (sweet, sweetly).

20. We all felt (happy, happily) after winning the game.

Remember that adjectives modify nouns, and in special cases, verbs. Adverbs, however, can modify adjectives, other adverbs, as well as verbs. Adverbs are often used to intensify the meaning of adjectives or other adverbs. Here, they have the meaning of *extremely*.

> याद रखें कि विशेषण संज्ञा को संशोधित करते हैं ,और खास प्रकरण में क्रिया को भी संशोधित करते हैं | जबकि क्रिया-विशेषण विशेषण , क्रिया-विशेषणों और क्रियाओं को भी संशोधित कर सकते हैं |
> क्रिया-विशेषण आम तौर पर विशेषण या अन्य क्रिया -विशेषण अर्थ को बढाने के लिए उपयोग किये जाते हैं | यहाँ उनका मतलब "extremely (अत्यधिक) " होता है |

For example:

I read a *very interesting book.*

Notice an adverb is used to intensify an adjective that modifies a noun.

He *ate extremely quickly.*

Notice the adverb is used to intensify another adverb that modifies a verb.

Keeping this in mind will help you make decisions between tricky adjective-adverb pairs, such as *real* and *really, high* and *highly, considerable* and *considerably,* and *extreme* and *extremely.*

EXERCISE SWE-59

Directions: Analyze the following phrases and circle the correct adjective or adverb form.

1.   appeared (extreme, extremely) beneficial

2.   was (high, highly) amused

3.   seemed (extreme, extremely) happy

4.   (extreme, extremely) heat

5.   is (high, highly) recommended

6.   (real, really) wonderful book

7.   a (real, really) diamond

8.   (extreme, extremely) amusing movie

9.   very (original, originally) idea

10.   felt (extreme, extremely) pleasure

Compare the following: *extreme heat* but *extremely hot*. Notice an adjective modifies a noun while an adverb modifies an adjective.

As you try to improve your writing skills, you might want to keep these structures in mind. Especially the **adverb-adjective-noun** structure. You see, using this easy structure it is possible to create some rather interesting combinations that are difficult to express using only adjectives. For example, let's say you want to describe some aspect of a restaurant, maybe a dining room. You might come up with something such as the ***warmly noisy dining room***. That captures a special feeling: it describes a comfortable level of sound. You can get pretty complicated here also, like the ***unobtrusively grandiloquent*** *dining room!* Try to include some of these structures in your writing. They're really not difficult. Can you come up with a few interesting combinations?

We'll finish the **WF** section and STEP THREE with a brief study of comparative and superlative forms. Every adjective has three forms: a base, comparative, and superlative form. The comparative is used to compare two people or things while the superlative is used with three or more.

प्रत्येक विशेषण की तीन अवस्थाएँ होती हैं – मूल, तुलनात्मक ,सर्वोत्कृष्ट । तुलनात्मक अवस्था दो मनुष्यों या वस्तुओं की तुलना करते समय उपयोग की जाती है । जबकि सर्वोत्कृष्ट का उपयोग तीन या उससे अधिक वस्तुओं के लिए होता है ।

There are a few irregular comparative and superlative forms, such as *good, better, best* and *little, less, least.* Most adjectives, however, follow the following patterns in the comparative and superlative forms.

NOUN	ONE SYLLA-BLE	TWO SYLLA-BLES OR MORE	TWO SYLLABLES ENDING WITH Y
ADJECTIVE	long	interesting	funny
COMPARATIVE	longer	more inter-esting	funnier
SUPERLATIVE	longest	most inter-esting	funniest

Note: some adjectives are "absolute" in meaning and should not be used in comparative or superlative forms. These include words such as *dead, perfect,* and *wrong.*

EXERCISE SWE-60

Directions: Fill in the blanks with correct comparative and superlative forms.

NOUN	COMPARATIVE	SUPERLATIVE
1. happy		
2. obscure		
3. wise		
4. generous		
5. messy		
6. good		
7. long		
8. funny		
9. interesting		
10. green		
11. bad		
12. beautiful		
13. fast		
14. comfortable		
15. great		
16. strange		
17. irregular		
18. careful		
19. lazy		
20. crazy		

Remember, the **comparative form** is used only for *two*, the **superlative** form for *three or more.*

EXERCISE SWE-61

Directions: Choose and circle the correct comparative or superlative form.

1. This dessert is the (more delicious, most delicious) I've ever eaten.

2. Of the two pairs of shoes, I like this one (more, the most).

3. Melissa's understanding of computers is (better, best) than mine.

4. Of the two gymnastic routines, the latter was the (better, best).

5. Eric is the (taller, tallest) child in the kindergarten.

6. The longer she waited the (more, most) she cried.

7. This exercise is (less, least) difficult than the first one.

8. A beam of light travels much (faster, fastest) than a speeding bullet.

9. English was my (easier, easiest) subject in elementary school.

10. Compared (to, with) most other students, Rafael is extremely smart.

11. The longer he skied the (more exhausted, most exhausted) he became.

12. Even though you didn't study, try to do your (better, best) on the test.

13. My brother is the (taller, tallest) person in our family.

14. Nick wanted to buy the (better, best) stereo he could find.

15. This paperback edition is (less, least) expensive than that hardback one.

Notice that *compared to* is used to show equality or similarity while *compared with* is used to point out difference. It might help you remember by studying the following. Notice that the equal sign, which represents similarity or equality has two marks, while the word *to* has two letters. *With,* of course has more than two letters, like the unequal sign. It is often useful to formulate a mental association as this one to help you remember details.

Compared *to*	=
Compared *with*	≠

Let's finish this section with a Mini-TOEFL practice exercise.

MINI TOEFL-16

Directions: In questions 1-5, choose the one word or phrase that best completes the sentence. In questions 6-10, identify the underlined word(s) that should be changed to make the sentence correct. **TIME: 6 minutes**

_____ 1. Of the two books written on the subject, this one is the _____ .

    (A) best   (B) worst
    (C) most complete   (D) better

_____ 2. Of all the many babies in the nursery, ours is the _____.

    (A) prettiest   (B) more pretty
    (C) prettier   (D) most pretty

_____ 3. Mrs. Goodman was on the floor looking _____ for her diamond ring.

    (A) careful   (B) carefully
    (C) for carefully   (D) searching

_____ 4. This book of short stories includes several _____.

    (A) real interesting tales
    (B) interesting really tales
    (C) really interesting tales
    (D) really interested tales

_____ 5. Of all the piano students, Benjamin is _____ advanced.

   (A) the more   (B) most
   (C) more   (D) the most

_____ 6. <u>Most</u> teachers and researchers <u>regular visit</u> univer-
         A   B
         sity libraries <u>to stay</u> abreast of new developments
                        C
         within their particular <u>fields of study</u>.
                                 D

_____ 7. <u>Although</u> he <u>has comparative</u> few contacts in the
         A   B
         music industry, Roger <u>is hoping his</u> rock band
                               C
         <u>will find</u> a producer for a new CD.
         D

_____ 8. <u>Although</u> the teacher agreed that the thesis was
         A
         written in a concise <u>and succinct</u> format she
                              B
         <u>was not convinced</u> that the subject had been
          C
         <u>adequately covered</u>.
          D

_____ 9. The sweet, <u>elderly couple</u> strolled <u>lazy</u>, hand-in-
                    A   B
         hand through the garden as they <u>had done</u> for
                                         C
         <u>some</u> fifty years.
          D

_____ 10. <u>The head</u> of the English <u>departmental</u> will make a
         A   B

decision <u>on</u> including the TOEFL exam
         C

<u>as a requirement</u> for completion of language
          D

studies.

POP QUIZ

Why can't soup smell *well?*

What's the difference between *compared to* and *compared with?*

How do you tell the difference between *ly* adjectives and *ly* adverbs?

What British pop group recoded *A Little Respect* and *Chains of Love?*

5-Step
TOEFL Prep
for Hindi Speakers

QUICK CHECK
Grammar Problem Areas

STEP ONE

MC	Main Clause
SC	Subordinate Clause

STEP TWO

S=V	Subject-Verb Agreement
S=P	Subject-Pronoun Agreement
VTF	Verb Tense or Form
PFR	Pronoun Form or Reference

STEP THREE

VBL	Verbals
WF	Word Form

STEP FOUR

>	WO	Word Order
	PS	Parallel Structure
	UR	Unnecessary Repetition

STEP FIVE

CU	Correct Usage

Word Order

Subject-Verb Inversion

Direct vs. Indirect Questions

EXERCISE SWE-62

Directions: Using the abbreviations that identify each type of error, classify the following ten errors, then try to correct the errors. Only ten of the twelve types of errors are listed.

CU 1. The caged birds begin 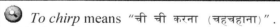 chirping when the sun raises.

WO 2. Under the house the old furniture is stored.

UR 3. Cherry trees are trees that fill Washington D.C. with flowers in April.

SC 4. The pie which was cooked by Jan who loves to cook.

S=P 5. Everyone should help themselves to drinks and hors d'oeuvres.

PFR 6. The surgeon which did the operation was highly recommended.

VBL 7. Cindy cut her foot on the breaking glass on the kitchen floor.

 To chirp means "ची ची करना (चहचहाना)".
This is called onomatopoeia—using words that imitate a sound. Did you know that the animals make different sounds in English than in Hindi? Of course, they really make the same sound. It is our interpretation of the sound that varies. For example, in English the rooster says, "Cocka-Doodle-Doo". What are some other animals whose sounds are expressed differently?

S=V   8. Five million dollars were a lot of money to win in the lottery.

WF   9. School desegregating remains a complicated issue for politicians.

PS   10. Swimming, jogging, and to play tennis are good forms of exercise.

Most of our study of **WO** errors will involve subject-verb inversion. Keep in mind that in normal word order we have:

SUBJECT + VERB + OBJECT

For example, **Nick ate a hamburger**.

However sometimes it is necessary to put the verb (sometimes an auxiliary verb) before the subject. This is what we mean by subject-verb inversion.

For example, **Down came the rain**.

Notice that the verb *came* is placed before the subject *rain*.

For many students, inverted word order is very difficult. When we learn a second language we usually learn *one* way, usually the easiest way, to express an idea. It is unusual that we go back and look for several **alternative ways** of expressing the same idea. Here, there will always be an easier, non-inverted way to express the idea, and most of us like to stick with this easier way because we're more accustomed to it.

In fact, using inverted order might feel somewhat strange to some. Try to learn to express ideas in an inverted form and include them more often in your normal speech patterns. You will sound much more fluent in English—a native speaker will use these inversions without even thinking about it. Try to apply the seven rules that follow to subject-verb inversion.

RULES FOR SUBJECT-VERB INVERSION

1.   If you begin a sentence with a **negative word** (or expression) or *only* **with a time expression**, you must use inverted order.

अगर आप वाक्य की शुरुवात एक नकारात्मक शब्द (या भाव) से या सिर्फ समय भाव से शुरू करते हैं तब आपको हमेशा उलटे क्रम में वाक्य बनाना चाहिए ।

Negatives include words and phrases such as: *never, hardly, seldom, at no time, not only, nowhere,* etc. Some examples of *only* with a time expression include: *only once, only after he graduated from college, only on Saturdays.*

If you begin a sentence with any of these words or phrases, they must be followed by: **AUX. VERB + SUBJECT + MAIN VERB**. For example, **Never has air pollution reached such dangerous levels** and **Only once have I skied**. Can you read these sentences, changing them to their non-inverted forms? It's easy—just start with the subject. They mean exactly the same in their inverted forms.

Perhaps the word order is not so difficult here as recognizing the negative word or phrase. Many negatives don't look so obviously negative as *never*. If you're not sure if you have a negative or not, try applying the question *How Frequently?* Negatives (as well as "only" + time expressions) will answer this question (with a few possible exceptions, such as *nowhere,* which should appear obviously negative because of the word *no*). Also, be aware that the time expression after *only* might be only one word or a long phrase or clause. Make sure you get all the way to the end of the time expression before you begin the inversion of the subject and verb in the main clause.

NOTE: With the verb *to be* an auxiliary verb is not necessary. Just put the verb *to be* before the subject. Before continuing with the subject-verb inversion rules, let's work with negatives.

EXERCISE SWE-63

Directions: The following sentences, which are incorrect, begin with negative words or phrases or *only* with a time expression. Write them again, making corrections in the word order (don't change the first word or phrase).

1. Never the temperature has been so high in the month of April.

    Never has the temperature been so high in the month

    of April.

2.   Only once Damon has forgotten to do his English homework.

_____

_____

3.   Scarcely I had sat down for dinner when the phone rang.

_____

_____

4.   Only after he passed the TOEFL he did begin to study Chinese.

_____

_____

5.   Only once I have gone to a college football game.

_____

_____

6.   Never before I have seen so much pollution in the city.

_____

_____

7.   Nowhere the price of beef is more expensive than in Japan.

_____

_____

8.   Not only we went to the picnic, but we also stayed for the basketball game.

_____

_____

9.   Only in the morning the doctor does see patients.

_____

_____

10.   Rarely it snows in Atlanta.

_____

_____

11.   Only after doing extensive research the doctoral candidate began writing his dissertation on language acquisition.

_____

_____

12.   At no time the concert goers were allowed to stand in
        their chairs.

        _____

        _____

13.   Nowhere I have enjoyed shopping as much as in New
        York City.

        _____

        _____

14.   Only after practicing for hours she could play the Bach
        prelude.

        _____

        _____

15.   Only on Sunday the museums are free of charge in
        Mexico City.

        _____

        _____

SUBJECT-VERB INVERSION RULES CONTIUED

2. If you've already studied the **S=V** (subject-verb agreement) section, you might recall that the words ***there***, ***here***, and ***where*** do not function as subjects. When you begin sentences with these words you should put the subject after the verb. For example: *Here* are the **books** that you ordered.

> अगर आप वाक्य को there, here or where से शुरू करते हैं तो उददेश्य को क्रिया के बाद लिखना चाहिए ।

Inversion is also required if you begin a sentence with ***little***, ***such***, ***so***, or ***few***, unless they modify a noun (in which case the noun will immediately follow). For example: *Little did* **we** *know that a war had been declared*, but *Such* **behavior** *is not allowed*. In the second example, *such* modifies *behavior*, a noun.

> उलटक्रम तब भी अनिवार्य है अगर आप वाक्य की शुरुआत little, such, so, or few,से करते हैं , जब तक कि ये संज्ञा को संशोधित न करें (उस केस में संज्ञा उसके बाद आएगी)

You must also invert your subject and verb if you begin a sentence with an adverb such as *up*, *down*, *in* or *out*.

For example:

*Down* came the **rain**.

अगर आप अपने वाक्य को क्रिया विशेषण *up, down, in,* or *out* से शुरू करते हैं तब भी उददेश्य और क्रिया को उलटकर लिखें ।

You might have heard of a children's song about a little spider. The English version of this song. "Itsy Bitsy Spider", has quite a few inversions of this type. Hand motions are used to describe actions such as: *"down came the rain"*, *"out came the sun"*.

In review, subject-verb inversion is required when you begin sentences with: 1) *there, here,* or *where,* 2) *little, such, so* or *few,* or 3) *down, in, out, up,* etc.

EXERCISE SWE-64

Directions: The following sentences, which are incorrect, begin with special words found in Rule 2. Write them again, making corrections in the word order (don't change the first word or phrase).

1. Up the flowers came after several weeks of rain.

   _____Up came the flowers after several weeks of rain._____

2. So hungry the children were that they could hardly wait for dinner.

   _____

   _____

4. There many important reasons are for learning English well.

   _____

   _____

5.   Here the answers are to the last quiz.

_____

_____

6.   Little the boy does know that he has a very serious medical problem.

_____

_____

7.   In the judge walked as everyone in the courtroom rose.

_____

_____

8.   Such is a desire to win not healthy.

_____

_____

9.   Few include literary works such details as those of James Joyce.

_____

_____

10. Up the smoke rose from the burning building.

_____

_____

11. Out the children ran from the school when the bell sounded.

_____

_____

12. So clever the thief was that the police never found him.

_____

_____

13. Such are animals common in Africa.

_____

_____

14. Here the books are that you asked me to find in the library.

_____

_____

15.   So was she talented that she was invited to perform at
       Carnegie Hall.

       _____

       _____

16.   Few the nights were that she didn't have a migraine
       headache.

       _____

       _____

Before we continue with the rules for subject-verb inversion,
let's do a Mini TOEFL practice exercise.

MINI TOEFL-17

Directions: In questions 1-5, choose the one word or phrase that best completes the sentence. In questions 6-10, identify the word(s) that should be changed to make the sentence correct. **TIME: 6 minutes**

_____ 1. Not until George finished his degree _____ to study Japanese.

(A) did he begin   (B) he began
(C) does he begin   (D) he did begin

_____ 2. Only after many weeks of gradually lowering his nicotine consumption _____ stop smoking for good.

(A) James could   (B) James did
(C) did James   (D) he did

_____ 3. Down _____ the moment we realized that we had forgotten our umbrella.

(A) the rain came   (B) the rain comes
(C) was the rain   (D) came the rain

_____ 4. So _____ that he collapsed at the end of the race.

(A) tired was the runner
(B) was the runner tired
(C) the runner was tired
(D) tired the runner was

_____ 5. Here _____ that you asked me to find.

   (A) the file is   (B) the files are
   (C) is the file   (D) did the file is

_____ 6. Here <u>the tools are</u> that <u>we will</u> need <u>to plant</u>
                    A   B   C
   our new <u>flower garden</u>.
              D

_____ 7. Only after the businessman <u>could provide</u>
                                         A
   <u>sufficient identification</u> to embassy
                B
   <u>staff members</u> <u>he was</u> issued a new passport.
          C   D

_____ 8. So heavy <u>the boxes of books were</u> that
                            A
   <u>it took</u> two men to carry <u>them from</u> the deli-
      B   C
   very truck <u>to the</u> library office.
                  D

_____ 9. Not until <u>recent</u> <u>has the use</u> of debit cards
                        A   B
   <u>become popular</u> among consumers who feel
          C
   they are safer and <u>more practical</u> than cash.
                              D

_____ 10. Only after you <u>have taken</u> a practice TOEFL
                              A

exam <u>we can</u> determine your level and decide if
                B

<u>you're ready</u> to begin <u>preparation classes</u>.
        C   D

SUBJECT-VERB INVERSION RULES CONTINUED

3.   Invert the subject and verb when beginning a sentence
with **the main verb of a passive verb structure**. For example:
*The bank robbers **were seen** running away* could also be written as ***Seen** running away **were** the bank robbers*. You often
hear this type of structure in news reporting. It puts more em-
phasis on the action.

निष्क्रिय क्रिया संरचना की मुख्य क्रिया से वाक्य शुरू करने पर भी
विषय और क्रिया को उलट कर उपयोग करना चाहिए ।

4.   Invert the subject and verb in **conditional sentences
that do not begin with the words** *if* or *unless*. For example:
If he had known, he would have come could also be written as
***Had** he known, he would have come*. The meaning in both
sentences is exactly the same.

प्रतिबंधित वाक्य जो *if* or *unless* से शुरू न हो रहे हो, उनमे भी विषय
और क्रिया को उलट कर उपयोग करना चाहिए ।

5. Invert the subject and verb if you begin a sentence with **a phrase which describes a location**. For example: *Several books are in the box* could also be written as *In the box* **are** several books.

अगर आप वाक्य की शुरुआत किसी स्थान को वर्णित करने वाले वाक्यांश से कर रहे हैं विषय और क्रिया को उलट कर उपयोग करना चाहिए ।

EXERCISE SWE-65

Directions: The following sentences, which are incorrect, begin with special words found in Rules 3, 4, and 5. Write them again, making corrections in the word order (maintain the first word or phrase).

1. Had known he about the party he would have come.

   Had he known about the party he would have

   come.

2. Under the table my shoes are.

   _____

   _____

3.   Seen at the awards presentation several movie stars were.

_____

_____

4.   Somewhere over the rainbow a pot of gold is.

_____

_____

5.   Discovered in the basket a kitten was.

_____

_____

6.   Should go he, James will certainly enjoy the concert.

_____

_____

7.   Around the corner my grandmother lives.

_____

_____

8.   Engaged to be married the happy couple was.

_____

_____

9.   Had read he the newspaper, he would have known about the fire.

_____

_____

10.   At the top of the mountain the skiers waited.

_____

_____

11.   Accused of the crime three teenagers were.

_____

_____

12.   Stored in the big trunk the little boy's toys are.

_____

_____

13.   In the trunk of the car the spare tire is.

_____

_____

14.   Should see you it, please buy it for me.

_____

_____

15.   Placed at the top of the Christmas tree the star was.

_____

_____

On the TOEFL exam you might find a structure that *should be* inverted and is *not*, but you might also find a structure that *is inverted* and *should not be*. Be especially careful with direct and indirect questions. In a direct question, such as *What is your name?*, inversion is required. However, inversion is not used in indirect questions, such as *I don't know **what your name is**.*

Notice that in a direct question you are actually asking a question and expecting an answer, while in an indirect question you only give reference to the fact—you're not asking for an answer. The next exercise will give you some practice with direct and indirect questions. Remember that in a direct question you invert, in an indirect question you do not invert.

EXERCISE SWE-66

Directions: Examine the word order in the following sentences. In the blanks put (**D?**) for **direct questions** and (**I?**) for **indirect questions**.

   D?   1. where did you go

_____ 2. what did you say

_____ 3. where James has been

_____ 4. how long does it last

_____ 5. what time it is

_____ 6. why Ann is on the floor

_____ 7. where he should turn

_____ 8. which he will choose

_____ 9. where James and Ann are

_____ 10. how do you feel

_____ 11. what color the walls are

_____ 12. why Monica didn't come home

_____ 13. where the bank is

_____ 14. why is she here.

_____ 15. why she left

_____ 16. are you sick

_____ 17. when they are arriving

_____ 18. how long will the movie last

_____ 19. which book he read

_____ 20 why James, Ann, and Monica are laughing

Now let's practice with some complete sentences that contain indirect questions that are incorrectly written as direct questions (they use inverted order when they should not).

EXERCISE SWE-67

Directions: Rewrite the following incorrect sentences, correcting the word order in the underlined part.

1. The student asked <u>how did he do on the exam</u>.

   <u>The student asked how he did on the exam.</u>

2. Do you know what kind of weather <u>will we have to-morrow</u>?

    _____

    _____

3. We are not sure <u>when will we return from our trip to Europe</u>.

    _____

    _____

4. Please tell me <u>how much money can I borrow</u>.

    _____

    _____

5. No one knew <u>why was the alarm sounded</u>.

    _____

    _____

6. Don't tell me <u>how did the movie end</u>.

    _____

    _____

7.   I'm not sure <u>how much postage does the letter need</u>.

_____

_____

8.   The report never said <u>where did the event take place</u>.

_____

_____

9.   I must find out <u>how much does the book cost</u>.

_____

_____

10.   I can't predict <u>what will the final score be</u>.

_____

_____

We need to review just a couple of small details to finish the **WO** section.

First, put adjectives *after* words that end in *one, body*, or *thing* (adjectives normally precede nouns in English). For example: *something* **wonderful**, not **wonderful** *something*.

Second, put nouns *after* the word *enough* (all other parts of speech precede this word). For example: **tall** *enough*, but *enough* **money**.

We'll end the **WO** section with a Mini TOEFL practice exercise.

MINI TOEFL-18

Directions: In questions 1-5, choose the one word or phrase that best completes the sentence. In questions 6-10, identify the word(s) that should be changed to make the sentence correct. **TIME: 6 minutes**

_____ 1. There _____ for us to continue waiting if the tickets are sold out.

    (A) no reason is   (B) reason no is
    (C) is no reason   (D) are no reason

_____ 2. At the end of the avenue _____ which serves great sandwiches.

    (A) a nice restaurant is
    (B) be a nice restaurant
    (C) was a nice restaurant
    (D) is a nice restaurant

_____ 3. _____ about the meeting I'm sure he would have come.

    (A) Had he known   (B) He had know

    (C) Known had he   (D) If he had

_____ 4. Only after getting her driver's license _____.

    (A) she was allowed to drive

    (B) was allowed to drive

    (C) was she allowed to drive

    (D) was allowed she to drive

_____ 5. Never _____ such rainy weather in February.

    (A) have we experienced

    (B) experienced have we

    (C) we have experienced

    (D) have been experienced

_____ 6. Only after raising funds for nearly two years
                            A

the club was capable of financing the expensive
        B   C   D

project.

_____ 7. At the edge of the coral reef a small shark was,
        A   B

although none of the lifeguards noticed it.
    C   D

_____ 8. Down <u>came the rain</u> so <u>heavy</u> that it caused
                 A   B

       <u>severe flooding</u> in several parts of the city and
               C

       stranded <u>numerous motorists</u>.
                    D

_____ 9. So good <u>her memory was</u> that Jane
                   A

       <u>almost never forgot</u> <u>someone's</u> name <u>or</u> telephone
              B   C   D

       number.

_____ 10. <u>Bored</u> with trying <u>to meet</u> <u>new someone</u> at a
          A   B   C

       nightclub, Bob decided <u>to try</u> the Internet chat
                              D

       sites.

5-Step
TOEFL Prep
for Hindi Speakers

QUICK CHECK
Grammar Problem Areas

STEP ONE

MC	Main Clause
SC	Subordinate Clause

STEP TWO

S=V	Subject-Verb Agreement
S=P	Subject-Pronoun Agreement
VTF	Verb Tense or Form
PFR	Pronoun Form or Reference

STEP THREE

VBL	Verbals
WF	Word Form

STEP FOUR

WO	Word Order
> PS	Parallel Structure
UR	Unnecessary Repetition

STEP FIVE

CU	Correct Usage

Parallel Structure

Series

Correlative Conjunctions

Comparisons

EXERCISE SWE-68

Directions: Using the abbreviations that identify each type of error, classify the following ten errors, then try to correct the errors. Only ten of the twelve types or errors are listed.

WF   1.   Mathematics was my easier subject in high school.

PFR   2.   Me receiving a perfect score came as a surprise.

VBL   3.   Steamed vegetables retain more nutrients than boiling ones.

VTF   4.   By the end of the week, we will finished our final projects.

SC   5.   The snack bar is closed for a few days so that can be remodeled.

CU   6.   Most generic brands have much of the same characteristics as name brands.

PS   7.   Included among his bad habits are smoking, drinking, and to eat excessively.

UR   8.   The students prefer the new computer registration because it is fast and rapid.

S=V   9.   *The New York Times* run the book reviews every Sunday.

MC   10. Although illegal in many countries, abortion it is practiced in the United States.

Let's begin the parallel structure (**PS**) section of our program. Remember that we must maintain a certain balance in formal English sentences. This will often be tested by presenting a series. All parts of the series, which is almost always separated by commas, should use the same grammatical structure. In other words, don't mix parts of speech that are included in a series.

GOOD PS: He likes to paint, to sing, and to play the piano.

BAD PS: He likes to paint, to sing, and playing the piano.

GOOD PS: She is young, intelligent, and beautiful.

BAD PS: She is young, intelligent, and she looks beautiful.

GOOD PS: Please do your work quietly, carefully, and quickly.

BAD PS: Please do your work quietly, in a careful manner, and quickly.

When all of the elements of a series are in the same grammatical form, we have good **parallel structure**. When some part is different we do not. This is one of the easiest errors on the TOEFL (and it is fairly frequently tested). When you notice commas separating elements of your sentence, always check the **PS** to make sure everything is in the same form. Avoid mixing structures. You might find a **PS** error that incorrectly mixes phrases with clauses, adjectives with adverbs, gerunds with infinitives, etc.

कई वाक्यों में एक क्रम होता है (ये सामान्यतया अर्ध विराम से विभाजित होते है) क्रम के प्रत्येक भाग की व्याकरण एक समान होनी चाहिए ।

EXERCISE SWE-69

Directions: All of the following sentences contain errors in parallel structure. Find the part of the sentence that is not parallel and underline it. Then write the correct form above it.

                                       to receive
1.   Do you believe it is better to give than <u>receiving</u>?

2.   I can offer you a glass of water, a wine, or a cup of coffee.

3.   Most New York City tourists like attending Broadway shows, to eat in China Town, and shopping at Saks Fifth.

4. She is extremely successful because of her intelligence, because of her integrity, and because she works very hard.

5. You should check all the verbs for correct tense, agree, and form.

6. The household chores I hate the most are vacuuming the carpet, to wash the dishes, and dusting the furniture.

7. At our university you can study pharmacology, medical, or dentistry.

8. You may choose to make your payments in two, sixth, or twelve monthly payments.

9. Most new college quarterbacks are conscious of, interested, but frightened by their duties as the team leader.

10. The couple bought the new furniture because it was on sale, because they liked the style, and because of its comfort.

11. Good students study frequent, carefully, and consistently.

12. The kindergarten children are learning to read, to write, and doing simple math problems.

13. The meal was simple, sophisticated, and enjoyably.

14. At the football camp the players were taught to kick, to pass, and tackling.

15. Santa Clause does not reward children who cry, pout, or misbehaving.

We must also pay attention to the parallel structure when sentences contain correlative conjunctions. These include structures such as: *either...or, neither...nor,* and *not only...but also.* The words that follow both parts of the correlative conjunction should be in the same grammatical form. For example, if you have an adjective after *not only* you should also have an adjective after *but also.*

जब वाक्य में सहस्वंधित संयोजक हो तो, संयोजक के पहले भाग के बाद में आने वाले शब्द , संयोजक के दूसरे भाग के बाद में आने वाले शब्दों के समांतर होने चाहिए ।

EXERCISE SWE-70

Directions: Each of the following sentences includes correlative conjunctions. Check the parallel structure and write **OK** if the sentence is correct or an (**X**) if it is wrong.

__OK__ 1. Books are generally classified as either fiction or non-fiction.

_____ 2. She not only plays the trumpet but also the trombone.

_____ 3. Neither rain nor snow will delay the delivery of the mail.

_____ 4. The water in the Dead Sea is not only salty but also contains concentrations of other minerals.

_____ 5. When appraising the value of a diamond one should consider not only the cut but also the clarity and color.

_____ 6. The Banyan tree, a member of the mulberry family, commonly grows in either eastern India or near Malaysia.

_____ 7. The lucky winner not only receives a new car but also a motorcycle.

_____ 8. The psychiatric patient was not only paranoid but also felt nervous.

_____ 9. For fastest service, you can make an appointment to take the TOEFL exam either by calling or faxing.

_____ 10. We hope to spend our summer vacation either in Paris or Rome.

We'll finish this **PS** section with a discussion of three types of errors in parallel structure that commonly occur when making **comparisons**.

1.   To maintain good parallel structure, try to compare things that are actually comparable. For example:

GOOD PS: The books used in the fifth grade class are much more difficult than *those* in the third grade class.

BAD PS: The books used in the fifth grade class are much more difficult than the third grade class. (You can't compare the books with the class).

GOOD PS: The director's salary is higher than his secretary's.

BAD PS: The director's salary is higher than his secretary. (You can't compare the salary with the secretary).

Try to make sure that you are comparing the right things and things that are actually comparable.

सही समांतर संरचना बनाये रखने के लिए तुलनीय तत्वों की ही तुलना करें ।

---

2.   When you compare a member of a group with the other members of the group, it is necessary to include words such as *any other* or *anyone else* (otherwise the sentence will not be logical). For example:

GOOD PS: Ed is smarter than anyone *else* in his family.

BAD PS: Ed is smarter than anyone in his family. (Ed is a member of the group *family* and he is not smarter than *himself*).

GOOD PS: The library is taller than any *other* building on campus.

BAD PS: The library is taller than any building on campus. (The library is a member of the group *buildings on campus* and it is not taller than *itself*).

Notice this works the same for people or objects.

किसी एक समूह के सदस्य की तुलना दूसरे समूह के सदस्य से करते समय else या *other* शब्द का उपयोग करें ।

3.   Do not eliminate words (even if they appear unimportant) when combining two comparisons in one sentence. Notice in the following example how two comparisons are correctly and incorrectly combined in one sentence.

First comparison: Ann's grades might be *better than* John's.

Second comparison: Ann's grades are *as good as* John's.

GOOD PS: Ann's grades are as good as if not better than John's.

BAD PS: Ann's grades are as good if not better than John's.

(Notice that the word *as* from the second comparison has been incorrectly eliminated).

When combining two comparisons in one sentence, don't eliminate any words from either comparison.

एक ही वाक्य में तुलनातमक पदों को जोड़ते समय , तुलनात्मक पद के किसी भाग को न हटाएं ।

EXERCISE SWE-71

Directions: Each of the following sentences contains comparisons. Check the parallel structure and write **OK** if the sentence is correct or an (**X**) if it is wrong.

__X__   1. The books on this shelf are priced much lower than that shelf.

_____   2. Disposable contact lenses are just as expensive if not more expensive than permanent lenses.

_____   3. Charles can play the trumpet better than anyone else in the marching band.

_____   4. The population of Tokyo is larger than that of New York City.

_____   5. Dick can run as fast if not faster than Jane.

_____   6. The administration building is taller than any building on campus.

_____   7. The operas of Mozart are more popular than Verdi.

_____   8. I can type just as well if not better than my sister.

_____   9. Albert, the school's star player, is taller than anyone on the basketball team.

_____   10. Tickets for this concert are more expensive than next week's.

_____ 11. Many argue that low tar cigarettes are just as dangerous as if not more dangerous than regular cigarettes

_____ 12. The Braves are better than any baseball team in the world.

_____ 13. The rate for our suites is higher than that of our single rooms.

_____ 14. Apples are just as nutritious as if not more nutritious than bananas.

_____ 15. Tania is a better writer than anyone else in her journalism class.

Now let's do an exercise that will provide a good review of all the **PS** points we have studied.

EXERCISE SWE-72

Directions: All of the following sentences are incorrect because they contain some type of **PS** error. Identify the errors and rewrite the sentences correctly in the blanks.

1.   A good typist works quick, accurately, and carefully.

      A good typist works quickly, accurately, and carefully.

2.   The apples on this tree are much redder than that tree.

      _____

      _____

3.   My blue jeans look much older than you.

      _____

      _____

4.   You should not only pick up a registration form but also a course list.

      _____

      _____

5.   Hawaii is more expensive to live in than any state in the U.S.

_____

_____

6.   We must decide where we will go and where to stay.

_____

_____

7.   This book is just as exciting if not more exciting than the author's first one.

_____

_____

8.   The damage caused by Hurricane Camille was greater than Eloise.

_____

_____

9.   Among her New Year's resolutions are to quit drinking, smoking, and to eat chocolate every day.

_____

_____

10.   The team lost because of inexperience and because they made many mistakes.

_____

_____

11.   The family not only swam but also playing tennis.

_____

_____

12.   Antique furniture is as expensive if not more expensive than modern furniture.

_____

_____

13.   To drop a course you must talk either to your counsel-
        lor or your department head.

        _____

        _____

14.   The band marches on the field, played several songs,
        and returned to their places in the stadium.

        _____

        _____

15.   More musical productions are staged in New York
        City than in any city in the world.

        _____

        _____

Let's finish the **PS** section of our program with a Mini TOEFL
practice exercise.

MINI TOEFL-19

Directions: In questions 1-5, choose the one word or phrase that best completes the sentence. In questions 6-10, identify the word(s) that should be changed to make the sentence correct. **TIME: 6 minutes**

_____ 1. The delay was caused either by mechanical problems _____ bad weather.

(A) or caused by   (B) or
(C) or by   (D) nor by

_____ 2. Students may choose from among several elective courses, including many art related courses such as _____ .

(A) painting, drawing, and sculpture
(B) to paint, drawing and sculpture
(C) how to paint, how to draw, and sculpture
(D) techniques of painting, basics of drawing, and to sculpt

_____ 3. This year's summer was _____ if not hotter than last year's.

(A) hot   (B) as hot
(C) hottest   (D) as hot as

_____ 4. During the vacation, I wanted to ski, _____, and to snow board.

(A) ice skating
(B) to ice skate
(C) to go ice skating
(D) ice skate

_____ 5. She was hired because of her experience and _____.

(A) because she is a hard worker
(B) because she works hard
(C) she works hard
(D) because of her hard work

_____ 6. The country's currency was devalued 🔍 because
     A   B

of an unstable Asian market and because
      C

investors reacted nervously.
      D

🔍Remember *because of* is followed by a phrase (no verb) while *because* is followed by a subordinate clause (with subject and verb). In this sentence, that rule affects what you can and cannot change. **Sometimes what is *not* underlined is just as important as what *is* underlined—what you *can't* change affects what you *must* change**.

_____ 7. The <u>political candidate</u> promised voters that he
              A
     <u>would fight</u> against <u>criminal,</u> poverty, and drugs if
              B   C
     <u>elected</u>.
              D

_____ 8. Compared <u>to most</u> schools, the military academy
              A
     that I <u>attended is</u> <u>more</u> disciplined, regimented,
              B   C
     and <u>difficult</u>.
              D

_____ 9. The <u>coach's assistant</u> is responsible not only
              A
     <u>for making</u> sure the team uniforms <u>are ready</u>
              B   C
     but also <u>keeps track</u> of the equipment.
              D

_____ 10. Wooden floors are just as <u>pretty</u> if not <u>prettier</u>
                                        A   B
     than <u>carpeted</u> or <u>tiled</u> floors.
              C   D

5-Step
TOEFL Prep
for Hindi Speakers

QUICK CHECK
Grammar Problem Areas

STEP ONE

MC	Main Clause
SC	Subordinate Clause

STEP TWO

S=V	Subject-Verb Agreement
S=P	Subject-Pronoun Agreement
VTF	Verb Tense or Form
PFR	Pronoun Form or Reference

STEP THREE

VBL	Verbals
WF	Word Form

STEP FOUR

WO	Word Order
PS	Parallel Structure
> UR	Unnecessary Repetition

STEP FIVE

CU	Correct Usage

Unnecessary Repetition

Synonyms

Verbs with Implication of More or Less

EXERCISE SWE-73

Directions: Using the abbreviations that identify each type of error, classify the following ten errors, then try to correct the errors. Only ten of the twelve types of errors are listed.

MC   1.   Is the constant horn blowing that bothers me most about being in a big city.

S=P   2.   The football crowd was so large that it took us half an hour to work through them and reach our seats on the top row of the stadium.

PS   3.   The misbehaved puppy chewed up my slippers, goes to the bathroom on the floor, and ran out the door and down the street.

VTF   4.   Yesterday Bobby swang on the rope and dropped into the creek at least fifty times.

S=V   5.   Everything, including the furniture, have been removed from the dilapidated house.

CU   6.   The mayor, city officials, and citizen representatives are discussing the issue between themselves.

VBL   7.   Although many still prefer importing wines, domestic varieties have been slowly increasing in popularity.

WO   8.   Why did he choose to live so far from home was never understood by his friends and family.

UR   9.   Quite often the university offers courses on various computer programs frequently.

SC   10. The book is on the top shelf belongs to my sister.

We'll finish STEP FOUR with a study of unnecessary repetition. Don't confuse **UR** errors for repeated subjects (discussed in the **MC** section). When you have an **UR** error, it means that words which have the same meaning have been used to describe the same thing in a sentence. Obviously, the better your vocabulary skills the easier it will be to avoid using words that have the same meaning. We'll start our study with a review of some common words with multiple meanings. Avoid using these words repetitively.

गैरजरूरी दोहराव से बचें , एक चीज़ के वर्णन के लिए केवल एक शब्द उपयोग करें तथा उसी के पर्यायवाची शब्दों का उपयोग न करें ।

EXERCISE SWE-74

Directions: After each of the following words, try to write at least two (more if possible) words which have the same meaning and would be repetitive if used together. A dictionary or thesaurus might be useful.

1.   easy   _____simple, basic, uncomplicated_____

2.   correct   _____

3.   pretty   _____

4.   large   _____

5.   total   _____

6.   initiate   _____

7.   fast   _____

8.   colorful   _____

9.   fancy   _____

10.   leap   _____

11.   moist   _____

12.   car   _____

13.   publicity _____

14.   look   _____

15.   seldom   _____

Some verbs in English have an implicit meaning of **more** or **less**. We should avoid using these verbs with the words *more* or *less*, as this would be considered unnecessary repetition. For example: *The store increased its prices by 15% **more**.* The word *more* is repetitive because *increase* has an implication of more.

कुछ क्रियाओं का अर्थ कम या अधिक होता है । उनका उपयोग *more* या *less* शब्द के साथ नहीं करना चाहिए।

EXERCISE SWE-75

Directions: Study the following list of verbs. If the verb has an implicit meaning of *more*, write (↑) in the blank. If the verb has an implicit meaning of *less*, write (↓) in the blank. If the verb has neither an implicit meaning of more nor an implicit meaning of less, write (=) in the blank.

↑	1.	increase	____	9.	regress
____	2.	improve	____	10.	reduce
____	3.	report	____	11.	research
____	4.	shrink	____	12.	diminish
____	5.	surpass	____	13.	expand
____	6.	enlarge	____	14.	deplete
____	7.	regulate	____	15.	inflate
____	8.	devalue			

EXERCISE SWE-76

Directions: Check the following sentences for unnecessary repetition. If the sentences are correct, write O**K** in the blank. If they are incorrect put an (**X**) in the blank.

  X   1.   You must repeat the lesson again.

_____ 2.   The concise and succinct report was well received.

_____ 3.   Explorers discovered and cultivated the new land.

_____ 4.   A car that is white in color stays cooler in the summer heat.

_____ 5.   Simultaneously, the students began protesting at the same time.

_____ 6.   The brief and impressive report revealed many new figures.

_____ 7.   We annually release our study every year.

_____ 8.   I won't guess or speculate about the outcome of the game.

_____ 9.   Law requires that you wear a motorcycle helmet on your head.

_____ 10. You should thoroughly read the instruction booklet in a complete manner.

_____ 11. We have installed an alarm system in the house and in the yard.

_____ 12. An eagle is the emblem and symbol of the country's flag.

_____ 13. Contaminated water has killed many fish and caused them to die.

_____ 14. Please select and examine five slides under the microscope.

_____ 15. Oak trees are trees that grow in old, hardwood forests.

As you have probably noticed, this is the shortest point of our five-step study of grammar—we've almost finished. After the following **Mini TOEFL**, we'll be finished with STEP FOUR and begin the final STEP FIVE, which includes correct usage **(CU)** errors.

MINI TOEFL-20

Directions In questions 1-5, choose the one word or phrase that best completes the sentence. In questions 6-10, identify the underlined word(s) that should be changed to make the sentence correct. **TIME: 6 minutes**

_____ 1. After the annual sale the department store planned to increase its prices _____.

(A) at 20%   (B) by 20% more
(C) by 20%   (D) higher

_____ 2. The well documented report was written in a short, _____ format.

(A) concise   (B) but complete
(C) succinct   (D) brief

_____ 3. Chocolate chip cookies are especially tasty _____ freshly baked.

(A) when   (B) and delicious
(C) and yummy when   (D) after

_____ 4. United States citizens have the _____ to "bear arms".

(A) constitutional right   (B) right constitution
(C) constitution right   (D) rightly constitution

5. The ducks in the park generally _____ near the edge of the lake where people often throw food to them.

   (A) staying   (B) they are staying
   (C) to stay   (D) stay

6. After swimming <u>for several</u> days with <u>minimum</u>
                A   B
   sleep, she become <u>fatigued and</u> exhausted and
                          C
   <u>eventually developed</u> leg cramps.
           D

7. <u>Even though</u> it is a law in most states for motorcy-
      A
   cle riders <u>to wear</u> helmets <u>on their heads,</u> some
             B   C
   <u>still do not seem</u> to take the law seriously.
         D

8. Sheep are <u>extremely valuable</u> to raise and
                A
   <u>profitable</u> to sell <u>in that its</u> provide people <u>with</u>
     B   C   D
   meat to eat and wool to wear.

_____ 9. The <u>moisture and</u> humidity in the greenhouse
               A
     <u>is carefully</u> maintained <u>at the proper level</u> all year
          B   C
     to insure maximum <u>growth potential</u> of all the
                             D
     plants.

_____ 10. Although the <u>English</u> professor <u>found</u> the
               A   B
     <u>student's short story</u> fascinating <u>and intriguing,</u> he
          C   D
     did not feel it met the required criteria.

POP QUIZ

Can you think of three words that mean

"नमी , उदासी", "तेज़", and "अच्छा" ?

5-Step
TOEFL Prep
for Hindi Speakers

QUICK CHECK
Grammar Problem Areas

STEP ONE

MC	Main Clause
SC	Subordinate Clause

STEP TWO

S=V	Subject-Verb Agreement
S=P	Subject-Pronoun Agreement
VTF	Verb Tense or Form
PFR	Pronoun Form or Reference

STEP THREE

VBL	Verbals
WF	Word Form

STEP FOUR

WO	Word Order
PS	Parallel Structure
UR	Unnecessary Repetition

STEP FIVE

> CU	Correct Usage

Correct Usage

Definite/Indefinite Articles

Make vs. Do

Problematic Verbs

Count and Non-count Nouns

EXERCISE SWE-77

Directions: Using the abbreviations that identify each type of error, classify the following ten errors, then try to correct the errors. Only ten of the twelve types of errors are listed.

VBL   1.   Growing up near the sea, surfing was Mark's favorite sport.

PS   2.   Robert not only studies the violin but also the cello.

WO   3.   Only after finishing her dissertation Rebecca did receive her Doctor's degree.

CU   4.   I travelled to Paris, Rome, and London, but the latter place was my favorite.

VTF   5.   Houdini, who died on Halloween, performs remarkable acts of escape.

PFR   6.   The person who I spoke with earlier suggested I call you.

SC   7.   If walk two miles south, you'll find the lake is a perfect spot for fishing.

S=P   8.   Everyone, including the senior students, must apply for their parking permit before the end of this week.

S=V   9. Both the lion and the tiger is in their houses.

WF   10. The poor girl has serious emotion problems as a result of many years of heavy drug use.

We're now ready to begin the final STEP FIVE of the SWE (Structure & Written Expression) section. This is an interesting point to study. Instead of a long, intensive study of one particular grammar point, we'll take a quick look at a variety of usage errors. This **CU** section will cover common idiomatic problems, problematic verbs, count and non-count words, make vs. do, etc. It's also a good idea to carefully study Appendix E, Common Usage Errors. If you're looking for material to review just days before taking the TOEFL exam, these are good areas to study. You can often pick up a few quick points by reviewing a variety of usage errors.

We begin with something fairly elementary—the use of **a** vs. **an**. In general this is just a matter of using **a** with a word which begins with a consonant sound, such as **book**, and **an** with a word which begins with a vowel sound, such as **apple**.

However, we must give special consideration to words beginning with three particular letters, as they can cause confusion, Those three letters are: **h**, **u**, and **o**.

Use **a** with all **h** words unless the **h** is silent, in which case you should use **an**. For example: a hurricane, a home, a horn but an honor, an honest face, an herb.

Use **a** with all **u** words that have a long **u** sound (such as the one heard in *tune*), but **an** with **u** words that have a short **u** sound (such as the one heard in *bug*). For example: a unicorn, a university, a union, but an umbrella, an unusual story, an umpire.

Use **an** with all **o** words (short or long sounds as found in *octopus* or *ozone*, respectively) but **a** with **o** words that have a **w** sound. For example, an orange, an odor, an original poem, but a one-story building, a once-familiar subject, a onetime event. Notice all the words with a **w** sound are formed with the word *one* or *once*.

Obviously, the correct use of these letters depends on correct pronunciation—even if you're not speaking aloud, you hear an internal pronunciation. We'll continue with an exercise that will give you some practice in pronouncing words and choosing between **a** and **an**.

EXERCISE SWE-78

Directions: Fill in the blanks with **a** or **an**.

1. __an__ orthopedic surgeon

2. _____ honorary degree

3. _____ one-eyed monster

4. _____ university degree

5. _____ house call

6. _____ half cup

7. _____ universal rule

8. _____ one-piece bathing suit

9. _____ one-sided argument

10. _____ honor student

11. _____ usual routine

12. _____ honest face

13. _____ only child

14. _____ unbelievable story

15. _____ herb garden

16. _____ union leader

17. _____ used car

18. _____ orange bicycle

19. _____ horror move

20. _____ house boat

Note: **a** and **an** are called indefinite articles, while **the** is a definite article. Let's take a look at a few rules for the use of definite and indefinite articles.

RULES FOR INDEFINITIVE ARTICLES A/AN

1.   The indefinite article **a** or **an** is used before singular count nouns (never with non-count or plural nouns) to mean "one". For example, a book, an offer, an umbrella, etc.

> अनिश्चित कालीन अनुच्छेद "a" या "an" का उपयोग एकवचन गणना संज्ञा (गैर गणना संज्ञा के साथ नहीं) जैसे कि "एक" के साथ किया जाता है .

2.   The indefinite article is used with certain numerical expressions. For example: a few, a lot, a hundred, a couple, a dozen, a pound, etc.

> अनिश्चित कालीन अनुच्छेद का उपयोग संख्यात्मक पदों में किया जाता है ।

3.   The indefinite article is used before time expressions to mean "per". For example: an apple a day, a mile a minute, $5 an hour.

> का उपयोग मात्रा –आवर्ती संबंध में किया जाता है ।

4.   The indefinite article is used before names of professions. For example: My mother is a doctor.

> एक अनिश्चित कालीन अनुच्छेद का उपयोग पेशे के नाम से पहले किया जाता है ।

The correct use of the definite article *the* is also often tested on the TOEFL exam. The rules for the definite article are a bit more complex than those for the indefinite article. Plus, you'll need to pay attention to when *not* to use it.

RULES FOR THE DEFINITE ARTICLE *THE*

1.   A definite article is used when both the speaker and the listener know what is being referred to. For example: Could you please close the window? (It is obvious which window).

2.   A definite article is used before expressions of time or position. For example: the morning, the present, the back, the top, the end.

3.   A definite article is used with singular nouns that represent larger classes of animals, parts of the body, musical instruments, etc. For example: The violin is a stringed instrument. The lungs are damaged by smoking.

4.   A definite article is used with ordinal numbers, but *not* with cardinal numbers. For example: The First World War, but World War Two. The fifth chapter, but Chapter Five.

5.   A definite article is used with decades, centuries, and general periods of time. For example: the 1930's, the fifties, the 20th century, the ages of rock and roll.

6.   A definite article is used with the superlative form of adjectives. For example: the tallest building, the most important decision.

7.   A definite article is used with the name of a nationality, but *not* before the name of a language. For example: The English love tea. English is spoken in Australia.

8.   A definite article is used with an adjective such as *poor, young, rich,* etc. to mean "people who are...". For example: Robin Hood stole from the rich and gave to the poor.

9.   A definite article is used when speaking about a specific noun, but it is *not* used when speaking in general terms. For example: I like pizza. I like the pizza at Pizza Hut.

10.   A definite article is used with official names of nations, states, and cities, but *not* with common names. It is also used before plural geographic names of lakes, mountains, and islands, but *not* before individual ones. For example: The United States of America, but America. The State of Texas, but Texas. The Rocky Mountains, but Mount Rushmore.

निश्चित अनुच्छेद का प्रयोग तब किया जाता है : 1) विधेय स्पष्ट हो 2) समय और दशा भाव के साथ 3) एकवचन संज्ञा के साथ अगर वह बड़े समूहों का सदस्य हो 4) क्रमसूचक संख्या के साथ , कार्डिनल अंको के साथ नहीं 5) दशकों , सदिओं और समय की सामान्य अवधि के साथ 6) सर्वोकृष्ट विशेषण के साथ 7) राष्ट्रीयता के नाम के साथ —पर भाषा के नाम के साथ नहीं 8) विशेषण जैसे "poor" या "young" जो लोगों की सामाजिक स्थिति बताते हैं 9) कुछ ख़ास नामों के साथ – सामान्य नाम के साथ नहीं 10) आधिकारिक नाम के साथ —आम नाम के साथ नहीं , भूगोलिक जगहों के बहुवचन नाम के साथ —प्रत्येक स्थान के साथ नहीं ।

Actually, there are even more rules for the use of the definite article, but these general rules should be enough for our purposes of TOEFL preparation. For a more detailed explanation you might consult an advanced English grammar handbook.

On the TOEFL exam you might find three types of errors involving definite and indefinite articles: 1. An incorrect use of a definite vs. an indefinite article (*a* instead of *an*, or *the* instead of *a* or *an*). 2. An incorrect inclusion or omission of an article—an article is included when it's not needed or omitted when it is needed. 3. An article used instead of a possessive—such as *the* instead of *its*.

Keep these types of errors in mind as you work through the following exercise and Mini TOEFL practice.

EXERCISE SWE-79

Directions: Practice using the correct articles by examining the choices in parenthesis and circling the correct one.

1. Spanish is (the most, most) widely spoken Romance language.

2. Sequoia, (a Cherokee, Cherokee) leader, created (the, a) first written form of North American Indian language.

3. Tongan is spoken (in, in the) Tongan Islands, (a, an) kingdom just west (of, of the) International Date Line.

4.   (A, The) Semitic languages, including Amharic, were introduced into Ethiopia from (a, the) Arabian Peninsula in (the, a) first millennium B.C.

5.   Kalmyk is spoken in (a, the) Russian Republic of Kalmykia, located just to (the west, west) of the Volga River, northwest (of, of the) Caspian Sea.

6.   The term "artificial language" refers to those, such as Esperanto, that have been created in (the hope, hope) that they might become (a, an) universal tongue.

7.   The spectacular advance (of, of the) English across (a, the) face of the world is (a, an) phenomenon without parallel in (the, a) history of language.

8.   Romany (is, is the) language (of a, of the) Gypsies who originally came from India.

9.   (Chinese, The Chinese) is spoken by more people than any other language in (a, the) world.

10.   Swedish is (most, the most) widely spoken of (a, the) Scandinavian languages, one branch of (a, the) Germanic languages.

MINI TOEFL-21

Directions: In questions 1-5, choose the one word or phrase that best completes the sentence. In questions 6-10, identify the underlined word(s) that should be changed to correct the sentence. **TIME: 6 minutes**

_____ 1. _____ desserts on our menu are extremely high in calories and not recommended for people that are on diets.

(A) The most   (B) None of the
(C) No   (D) Most

_____ 2. Witch doctors are famous for _____ mysterious herbal remedies.

(A) their   (B) the
(C) a   (D) an

_____ 3. The giant anaconda snake of South America can reach _____ of nearly 30 feet.

(A) length   (B) long
(C) a length   (D) an length

_____ 4. Although Orville Wright is known as _____ man to fly an airplane, his first flight flew only 12 feet off the ground and lasted only 12 seconds.

(A) a first   (B) first
(C) the first   (D) an first

_____ 5. _____ mountain in the North Carolina Blue Ridge
mountain range is called Grandfather Mountain.

(A) The highest   (B) A highest
(C) The higher   (D) An higher

_____ 6. A eclipse of the sun can be dangerous if viewed
              A   B   C
with the naked eye.
              D

_____ 7. New Year's Day, a first day of a new year, is
                        A   B   C
celebrated on various days around the world.
              D

_____ 8. The trapeze artist slowly climbed to top of the
                  A   B
rope and up to the platform where she would begin
                                               C
her spectacular performance of mid-air flips.
                                    D

_____ 9. The last chapter of the book was such a disap-
              A   B
pointment that I regretted having spent so many
                                  C   D
time reading the 300 pages.

_____ 10. It is not difficult to see the <u>solid</u> waste that is being
A

dumped <u>into the</u> river by <u>the paper company</u> be-
B   C

cause it floats <u>to surface</u> of the water.
D

Let's continue with something that gives many people problems—**make** and **do**. To make matters even more confusing
we use *do* as a normal verb and also as an auxiliary verb. For
our purposes here, however, we will only be considering *do* as
a normal verb as we try to distinguish between the two.

Deciding between which verb—*make* or *do*—to use is somewhat difficult. Most grammar books or TOEFL preparation
programs don't offer any rules. That's because their use is
idiomatic—they don't really follow rules but must be learned
by example, through experience. The use of these verbs does
not always seem logical: why *make* the bed and then *do* the
dishes?

What follows are not hard-fast rules, rather *guidelines* for the use of *make* and *do* which should help you make decisions most of the time. You might find an occasional exception, or a case that does not seem to fit neatly under any of the following guidelines.

Also keep in mind that *make* is used somewhat more frequently than *do*. If forced to guess, your chances are better with *make!* And like many points in **STEP FIVE**, you might see this on the TOEFL in the correct, not always the incorrect, form. Don't assume, in other words, that every time you see *make* or *do* (as well as other structures in this section) that it is the error. Perhaps it is actually correct and the error is hidden somewhere else in the sentence.

We continue with guidelines that describe situations that normally require the use of *make* or *do*.

GUIDELINES FOR *MAKE*

1. The first category of activities that normally requires the use of *make* relates to **sound**. You *make* a sound, a noise; a musical instrument *makes* a tone.

2. The next category involves **verbal communication**--ideas that can be communicated by speaking. You *make* a comment, a remark, a speech, a comparison, a suggestion, an announcement.

3. Use *make* for activities related to **planning**. You *make* plans, arrangements, and reservations.

4. *Make* is often used with a noun to replace a related verb. For example:

    discover = make a discovery
    offer = make an offer
    stop = make a stop
    turn = make a turn
    profit = make a profit

5. Use *make* with activities related to **achievement**--the result of work. You *make* progress, advances, a deal.

6. The final category of activities that will normally be used with *make* involves **creative construction**--to create, produce, or change something, often involving an element of creativity or imagination. You *make* a cake, a sculpture, a fire, a change.

GUIDELINES FOR *DO*

1. Use *do* for activities that are **habitual**--routine activities that you do over and over in the same way. We often use *do* as a substitute for other verbs, especially those referring to household chores. You *do* the dishes, the housework, the laundry, the ironing, the cleaning.

2. Use *do* for activities that are **academic** by nature. You *do* research, homework, exercises (the academic or physical type).

3. Use *do* for activities directly related to the routine of **work**. You *do* your work, a good job, business, your best.

4. Be aware that many phrasal verbs formed with *do* have special meanings (refer to the Appendix B, Phrasal Verbs). Notice the following examples: A vacation will *do* you good (improve your sense of well being or health). The picture does not *do* you justice (show you as attractive as you really are). The school decided to *do* away with the old computers (dispose of them).

5.   You probably won't see this on the TOEFL, because it's extremely informal and not grammatically correct. But just in case you hear it in a movie or on the street, we'll mention it. *Do* is sometimes used in special ways and might be considered sophisticated or snobbish. For example, you might hear. "Let's *do* lunch tomorrow." "Let's *do* the beach this weekend." Again, this is not correct, but you might hear it!

Study these guidelines and remember that in general we use *do* to focus on an activity and *make* on the result of the activity.

EXERCISE SWE-80

Directions: Examine the words in the box and then list them below in the *make* or *do* column.

an appointment	friends	homework
arrangements	a turn	money
the dishes	plans	the laundry
a tone	your best	research
a comparison	a speech	housework
an effort	a discovery	business
the bed	a proposal	a recommendation

MAKE	**DO**

PROBLEMATIC VERBS

We continue with what many grammar books call *problematic* verbs. Indeed, they are problematic—even for native speakers. These verbs include: *lie* and *lay*, *sit* ant *set*, *rise* and *raise*.

Why are these verbs so difficult? They are difficult for several reasons. First of all, the **conjugation** is confusing. Study the table that follows carefully. Obviously, it will not help to learn all of the rules for their correct usage if you don't know the correct conjugation. Notice that the present tense form *lay* is the same as the past tense form of *lie*. Notice the subtle difference between *lain* and *laid*, *lying* and *laying*, and *rising* and *raising*. These small differences in spelling make big differences in meaning.

The second reason they are difficult involves the **pronunciation**. It is true that you don't have to speak aloud when taking the TOEFL exam. However we still "hear" an internal pronunciation when we read words. "Hearing" them wrong can lead to making wrong decisions in their usage. For example, if you pronounce *raise* incorrectly, you might hear something like RAH-EEZ, which sounds more closely to *rise*.

The final difficulty is in **usage**. These verbs, while they follow certain patterns, can be confusing. It is necessary to practice with as many example situations as possible. Luckily, the use of these verbs is not frequently tested on the TOEFL. And again, don't assume that every time you see one of these words that it is automatically the error. It might be a decoy to cover up another error in the sentence.

It will help as you study the following conjugations if you think of these verbs in groups of *transitive* and *intransitive*. Transitive verbs take a complement, intransitive verbs do not.

INTRANSITIVE VERBS

SIMPLE	PAST	PAST PARTICIPLE	PRESENT PARTICIPLE
sit	sat	sat	sitting
lie	lay	lain	lying
rise	rose	risen	rising

TRANSITIVE VERBS

SIMPLE	PAST	PAST PARTICIPLE	PRESENT PARTICIPLE
set	set	set	setting
lay	laid	laid	laying
raise	raised	raised	raising

We will examine each of these individually, but keep in mind that *lie* and *sit* are similar in the same way that *lay* and *set* are similar. *Lay* and *set* express the idea of **to put** and will always have a direct object (you have to put something). *Lie* and *sit* express the idea of **to be**—a reference to position (or assuming that position).

Raise in general means to elevate (always with a direct object), while *rise*, in general, means to increase. But you'll need to study these more carefully and keep in mind that *raise* is used to describe action that is forced or voluntary while *rise* is used to describe action that is natural or involuntary.

You can study **sit** and **lie** together. They are probably the easiest to use. Again, they are intransitive and usually mean *to be*, the difference being *to be* in a seated or reclined position. *Lie* can also have the meaning of not telling the truth,

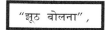

although the conjugations are different and there should never be much confusion between the two forms because they are so different in meaning.

Set and **lay** can also be studied together. They are transitive and always take a direct object. They have the meaning of **to put**—you use these meaning to put or place something. They can often be used interchangeably (you could *set* or *lay* a book on the table). However there are quite a few idiomatic differences where we must use one or the other.

<u>set</u>	<u>lay</u>
a watch or clock	your head on the pillow
a table	a baby on the bed
broken bones	"lay to rest"
"set out" plants	"lay off" employees
a medical condition "sets in"	bricks

Rise and **raise** can be studied together. Remember that *rise* is intransitive and never has a direct object. It means *increase* or *move up without help*. It is used for action that is *natural* or *involuntary*. *Raise* is transitive and always has a direct object. It means to *elevate* or *increase something*. It is used for action that is *forced* or *voluntary*.

The use of *rise* and *raise* does not always seem logical. For example, you *raise* your hand or leg, but if you stand up you *rise*. Be especially careful with anything related to money—inflation, prices, rent, etc. You might use *rise* or *raise*, depending on whether or not the action is natural or forced.

Note: Raise also has the meaning of

"बड़ा करना या पालना"

in reference to the upbringing of people or animals or

"उगाना या उपजाना"

in reference to plants; cultivating. The conjugations are the same.

raise	rise
the flag	the sun
your hand	to stand up
a question	smoke
your voice	wake up
$ (see above)	$ inflation, taxes, etc.

EXERCISE SWE-81

Directions: Circle the correct form of the verb in parenthesis.

1.   Make sure you ((set), sit) out the bulbs well before the arrival of spring.

2.   The delivery boy (lay, laid) the pizza on the table.

3.   If you're so tired, why don't you (lay, lie) down for a while?

4.   Hot air balloons work because hot air (raises, rises).

5.   The construction workers plan to (lay, lie) the bricks this afternoon.

6.   The court will come to order. All (raise, rise) for the honorable judge.

7.   The owner of the small candy store was forced to (rise, raise) her prices.

8.   Prices often (raise, rise) as a result of increasing un-employment levels.

9.   Carol was (raised, risen) in the Methodist church in a small town.

10.   The vice president was forced to (raise, rise) the ques-tion at the meeting.

11.   Her fear of cancer was (lay, laid) to rest by the doctor's kind words.

12.   Your broken arm will have to be (sit, set) in a cast.

13.   Avoid (sitting, setting) in the sun too long or you might burn your skin.

14.   The box has been (lying, laying) in the attic for many years.

15.   Students who work hard are able to (rise, raise) their TOEFL scores.

It is necessary in English to pay attention to words that are **countable** or **non-countable**, as well as countable words that refer to only two or to three or more people or things. For example, we must use *between* for two and *among* for three or more.

The following exercise will give you some practice with words that must be used only to refer to two or to three or more.
Note: some of the forms are comparative or superlative forms. Remember that comparative forms always refer to two, while superlative forms always refer to three or more.

EXERCISE SWE-82

Directions: Examine the following list of words. If they refer to two, write (**2**) in the blank. If they refer to three or more, write (**3+**).

__3+__	1.	all	_____	11.	either
_____	2.	inferior	_____	12.	better
_____	3.	both	_____	13.	least
_____	4.	neither	_____	14.	more
_____	5.	greater	_____	15.	between
_____	6.	among	_____	16.	former
_____	7 latter		_____	17.	worst
_____	8.	nicest	_____	18.	superior
_____	9.	none	_____	19.	most
_____	10.	Worse	_____	20.	best

 Be careful not to confuse **latter**, "पिछला"
with **later**, "के बाद".

Now let's move a little closer to the format of the TOEFL exam. Try to think logically—picture what you're describing. Also, watch out for traps (unrelated errors in sentences where one of these words referring to two or three or more is used correctly).

EXERCISE SWE-83

Directions: Examine the following sentences and try to identify the error. Write the letter (**A**) or (**B**) which corresponds to the error.

__A__   1. <u>All</u> of the tires on the bicycle <u>are</u> flat.
           A   B

_____   2. Of <u>all</u> the homes in this neighbourhood, mine
               A
          has the <u>more</u> beautiful lawn.
                 B

_____   3. <u>Neither</u> of the five <u>best</u> pieces will be on public
           A   B
          display.

_____   4. French and Arabic are spoken in Morocco, but the
          <u>former</u> is used <u>most</u> by the upper classes.
           A   B

_____   5. <u>Between</u> the waiters, chefs, and managers the
           A
          lunch shift is <u>more</u> popular than the dinner shift.
                    B

_____ 6. The fifth chapter of the book contained the <u>most</u>
A
important information but was also the <u>more</u>
B
boring.

_____ 7. The poor cat was blind in <u>both</u> of its eyes and deaf
A
in <u>all</u> of its ears.
B

_____ 8. Of the five problems addressed today, the <u>latter</u> is
A
by far the <u>most</u> serious.
B

_____ 9. The bilingual child spoke Chinese and English,

<u>both</u> of which <u>was</u> learned from a very early age.
A   B

_____ 10. Of the two puppies, the <u>oldest</u> was the <u>more</u>
A   B
active.

Just as we must be concerned with words that refer to only two or to three or more, it is necessary to concentrate on countable and non-countable nouns and words used to refer only to count, non-count, or to both count and non-countable nouns.

Remember that a count noun, by definition, has a plural form. You can put a number in front of it. For example, you can say *5 books* but not *5 water*. A non-countable noun has no plural form.

EXERCISE SWE-84

Directions: In the blanks write (**C**) for countable nouns or (**NC**) for non-countable nouns.

_NC_   1.   accounting

_____   2.   lumber

_____   3.   information

_____   4.   shelf

_____   5. money

_____   6.   respect

_____   7.   age

_____   8.   tooth

_____   9.   innocence

_____   10. employment

_____   11.   withdrawal

_____   12.   circumstance

_____   13.   sophistication

_____   14.   moisture

_____   15.   arrangement

_____   16.   vote

_____   17.   art

_____   18.   electricity

_____   19.   strawberry

_____   20.   job

> Some students have a hard time understanding why *money* is considered non-countable. *Money* is conceptual. What you actually count are the bills, "सिक्के" and coins, "हुंडी".

Now let's examine the differences in the use of words used with only count nouns, words used with only non-countable nouns, or both.

As you work through the following exercise, think of something countable such as "cookies" and something non-countable such as "milk"—for both count and non-countable, think of "cookies and milk".

EXERCISE SWE-85

Directions: In the blanks write (**C**) for words used only with countable nouns, write (**NC**) for words used with only non-countable nouns, and write (**B**) for words used with both countable and non-countable nouns.

__B__	1.	some	_____ 9.	both of
_____	2.	one, two, three...	_____ 10.	little
_____	3.	amount	_____ 11.	neither/either
_____	4.	the	_____ 12.	any
_____	5.	many	_____ 13.	several
_____	6.	quantity	_____ 14.	much
_____	7.	few	_____ 15.	none
_____	8.	less		

Now we'll see how these words might be tested in a format closer to the TOEFL exam. Again, watch out for tricks! Don't assume that the error involves a countable or non-countable noun.

EXERCISE SWE-86

Directions: Examine the following sentences and try to identify the error. Write the letter (**A**) or (**B**) which corresponds to the error.

B   1.   All of the rain that <u>fall</u> at the laboratory site is
          A   B
      is measured

_____ 2.   The <u>amount</u> of books in the library is more
            A
      important than the <u>number</u> of periodicals.
                      B

_____ 3.   There are <u>little</u> cookies and even <u>fewer</u> sandwiches
                A   B
      left for the guests.

_____ 4.   <u>A</u> water in the pool is so <u>heavily</u> chlorinated that
      A   B
      it burns my eyes.

_____ 5.   <u>Some</u> of the book <u>contain</u> material that might be
         A   B
      considered offensive to some readers.

_____ 6. <u>Much</u> plants are poisonous even though
       A
<u>they appear</u> lovely to the eye.
    B

_____ 7. <u>All</u> of the lifeguards are required to swim no <u>less</u>
    A   B
than 3 miles as a part of their intensive training.

_____ 8. <u>Many</u> of my work <u>was done</u> in the research
    A   B
library.

_____ 9. If you are concerned about the <u>quantity</u> of
                                 A
sugar in your diet you should consider drinking

<u>artificially sweetened</u> beverages.
    B

_____ 10. The <u>researcher</u> use <u>many</u> tests to draw their con-
      A   B
clusions.

We've almost finished with **STEP FIVE** and the Structure and Written Expression section of this program. Before you work through the next exercise and the final Mini TOEFL practice exercise, it is advised that you first study carefully Appendix E, Common Usage Errors. You'll find explanations to several errors that are found in this exercise.

EXERCISE SWE-87

Directions: Examine the following sentences and write **OK** in the blank if they are correct. If they have a usage error, put an (**X**) in the blank and underline and correct the error.

(further)
_X_ 1. <u>Farther</u> research is still needed to solve the mysteries of our solar system.

_____ 2. The counties effected by the hurricane were visited by the governor.

_____ 3. We are all ready to jump out of the airplane.

_____ 4. There seems to be a conflict among the doctors, nurses, and hospital administrators.

_____ 5. I often talk to my priest when I feel that I need sound advice.

_____ 6. There maybe a problem with your computer's monitor.

_____ 7. Please set down at the table so that dinner can be served.

_____ 8. We must be concerned with the amount of prisoners in our overcrowded jails.

_____ 9. Fruits like oranges, grapefruits, and lemons are a good source of vitamin C.

_____ 10. The president will give his address from the front steps of the capitol.

_____ 11. Its already time to make reservations for our beach vacation.

_____ 12. These kind of books are difficult to find and very expensive.

_____ 13. We have to decide weather we'll go to the game or just watch it on TV.

_____ 14. The student who's car was towed away will be very upset.

_____ 15. The weather today is pretty chilly and a little windy.

MINI TOEFL-22

Directions: In questions 1-5, choose the one word or phrase that best completes the sentence. In questions 6-10, identify the word(s) that should be changed to make the sentence correct. **TIME: 6 minutes**

_____ 1. _____ many factors to consider when choosing the right university.

(A) Their are   (B) There is
(C) They're   (D) There are

_____ 2. The little boy told his mother that he _____ watch TV than practice the violin.

(A) should   (B) would rather
(C) might   (D) had better

_____ 3. _____ of books were written for second year pre-med students.

(A) This kind   (B) These kinds
(C) That kind   (D) This sort

_____ 4. Small dogs _____ Pekinese, Poodles, and Chihuahuas make good pets for people with limited space.

(A) such as   (B) as such
(C) like   (D) as if

_____ 5. _____ will be necessary before conclusions can be drawn.

(A) Further informations
(B) Farther information
(C) Farther research
(D) Further information

_____ 6. It is better to <u>have less</u> students in a class <u>so that</u>
                             A   B
each student <u>might</u> get the individual attention
             C
from the teacher that <u>he needs</u>.
                       D

_____ 7. The university <u>intends</u> to conduct a <u>search</u>
                            A   B
involving several candidates before <u>reaching a</u>
                                     C
agreement <u>on the</u> new president.
          D

_____ 8. The students <u>who's names</u> are called <u>are requested</u>
                          A   B
to <u>make</u> an appointment this week with their
   C
faculty <u>advisors</u>.
        D

_____ 9. <u>Whether might</u> be described as any combination
          A
<u>of</u> various <u>amounts</u> of heat, <u>moisture</u>, and motion
B   C   D
in the air.

_____ 10. Compared <u>to the</u> last twenty winning seasons,
             A
<u>this year's</u> losing season <u>was an</u> <u>enormous</u>
     B   C   D
disappointment.

POP QUIZ

Do you *rise* or *raise* a question?

Do you *make* or *do* exercises?

Words beginning with which three letters might cause problems with the use of *a* and *an*?

Is *quantity* used with count or non-count nouns?

Written Essay

Taking a position

Organization of Essay

General Advice

Score Explanation

Sample Questions

Since the PBT (paper-based TOEFL) has been phased out and replaced with iBT (Internet-based TOEFL), and since there is no essay on the ITP (Institutional TOEFL), this supplement is included here especially for those taking this course as a pre-iBT program. On the iBT you will have to write an essay. In fact, you'll have to write two, an independent (based on your opinion) and an integrated (based on information drawn from a reading and listening source).

The following will help you organize a good independent essay, which requires a very formal essay structure with an introduction, body, and conclusion. This does not address the integrated essay. But keep in mind, you don't have to include this formal structure on the integrated; your essay will be organized into paragraphs that identify main points from a lecture you hear and make required connections to a related reading passage.

By taking time to study the organization and requirements of a good essay, you can greatly improve your ability to write an essay with limited practice. It is fairly **easy to improve** by following the advice in this program and writing a few practice essays before the actual exam. Careful study of the previous grammar section will also greatly improve your writing skills.

The first question most students have regarding this essay is: **How long should it be?** Really, the length of this essay is much less important than how well you take and support a position and write a well organized essay that demonstrates skill in writing correctly in English. Generally speaking, however, this is a rather short essay. Think in terms of five strong paragraphs consisting of three to five sentences.

TAKING A POSITION

Again, what you write is more important than how much you write. The first thing you should do is **choose your position**. Once you have done this, stick with it. Don't go back and forth on the issue unless you've specifically been asked to compare and contrast ideas. Remember, the people who grade your essay don't really care so much what your opinion is as how well you support it.

For example, suppose you've been asked the following question: **Do you prefer living in a big city or a small town?** Take a couple of minutes (the essay will be limited to 30 minutes) and make a decision—choose your position. Most likely you could think of reasons to support either side of this issue, but you must make a decision at this point.

ORGANIZING YOUR ESSAY

Once you're sure of your position, **choose at least three reasons** to support your position. Go ahead and try! Choose at least three reasons to support your position that you'd prefer to live in a big city or a small town. List them in the blanks below. Be brief—just 2 or 3 words should identify each reason. It's also possible to choose 4 or 5 reasons, depending on the complexity of the topic—try to limit your reasons to 5.

1. _____

2. _____

3. _____

This is perhaps the hardest part of writing an essay: choosing a position and supporting it with reasons. Now, you can easily organize your essay. If, however, you were not able to come up with at least three reasons to support your position, you really don't have much of a position to support. **You should reconsider your position**. It will be very difficult to write an acceptable essay if your position is not strong enough to be supported by three reasons.

ESSAY ORGANIZATION
Your essay should have three clearly defined parts:

I.   **Introduction Paragraph**
II.   **Body (1 to 3 paragraphs, minimum)**
III.   **Conclusion Paragraph**

As you write your essay, think of the shape of an hourglass. You want to start in broad, general terms. Then you narrow your writing to more 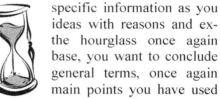 specific information as you support your general ideas with reasons and ex- amples. Then, just as the hourglass once again grows broader at the base, you want to conclude your essay in broad, general terms, once again briefly stating the main points you have used to support your position. The introduction and the conclusion are nearly identical.

Again: **begin broadly, get more specific in the body, and conclude broadly**.

For organizational purposes let's begin with the body of your essay. Remember those three points that support your position? These points should be strong enough to turn them into **topic sentences** that will begin the paragraphs of the body of your essay. Of course, every sentence that follows a topic sentence should be directly related to it and be supportive of it—don't include any sentences in this paragraph that are unrelated to your topic sentence. Go ahead. Take your three points and write out complete topic sentences.

1. _____

_____

2. _____

_____

3. _____

_____

Once you have your topic sentences ready to expand into paragraphs, take just a second and put them in the **best possible order**. Often a couple of your points may be stronger or weaker than the others—especially if you have more than three. You want to begin with what you feel is the strongest point—it's always good to start as convincingly as possible. Then save your second strongest point for last—it's also good to end strongly. Tuck the weaker point(s) in between.

After you write out the body paragraphs, go back and write your **introduction** paragraph. The first sentence, the topic sentence, should state your position. Clearly state your position, avoiding phrases like "In my opinion...", "After careful thought, it is clear to see..." In other words **avoid saying what you're going to say** and just say it. After the topic sentence, briefly state your reasons to support it—the same reasons that are used for the topic sentences in the body.

The **conclusion** is basically a repetition of your introduction. Again, restate the position you've taken and supported, perhaps by beginning with a word like "clearly" or "obliviously". Then, once again briefly restate your main points. In the very last sentence, find one more way to state the main position. You might use a clever quotation or rephrase the position in the form of a question. You could describe a conditional situation in which you choose an option..." If I had to choose between living in a city or a small town, I would not hesitate to choose..."

GENERAL ADVICE

The most important thing to remember when writing this essay, or anything for that matter, is your reader. **ALWAYS REMEMBER YOUR READER!** Don't make it difficult for your reader to understand what you've written. Don't assume any previous knowledge or expertise on the reader's part. Don't assume that the reader knows what you're thinking but never wrote. In short, take your reader by the hand and carefully walk him through your essay.

Never let him fall into the "deep water" of your unintelligible writing and "drown". Keep your sentences short and simple, even if you feel like you're writing on a third-grade level. You won't get extra points for complexity, but you'll certainly lose points if the reader can't understand what you're trying to say. This is the biggest problem most students have with this essay. **Short, concise sentences are better than long, complicated ones**.

Short and sweet! Some think it's a sign of a talented writer to write very lengthy sentences, with several transitions and numerous ideas. This is **not** considered a good writing style in English. It will keep the reader's attention if you mix really short sentences with longer ones, but avoid very long sentences completely. Try to use one idea per sentence. Don't go on and on and on and… Better, put a period, let the reader "breathe", and start a new sentence. Using a short sentence style will make it easier for you to express your ideas in an understandable way, which will certainly be easier for the reader to follow.

Remember, with just **limited practice** you can substantially improve your ability to write a good essay. Don't be afraid to try. You should write at least three complete essays before the actual exam.

Some **sample writing topics** follow—your teacher might assign a few of these to you to write outside of class. You can find more sample topics in the official TOEFL Bulletin. The following are quite typical of what you'll encounter on the real exam.

SAMPLE WRITING TOPICS

Let's begin with a topic you're already familiar with. Use the notes you made earlier and write out a complete essay for the following question number one. Don't worry about time on the first couple of essays. Once you get the structure right, then try to write future essays timed at 30 minutes, just like the real exam.

QUESTION NUMBER ONE

Do you prefer to live in a big city or a small town? Why? Support your opinion with specific reasons.

QUESTION NUMBER TWO

If you had to choose one thing to represent your country and *send* to an international symposium on culture, what would you choose. Why?

QUESTION NUMBER THREE

You must choose how your university should use a large grant of money. Would you use it: A) to buy computer equipment and software, B) to buy books for the library, or C) for general use in the athletic department? Choose only one option and support your answer with specific reasons.

QUESTION NUMBER FOUR

Do you think it's preferable for college students to live at home or on their own? Support your opinion with detailed reasons.

QUESTION NUMBER FIVE

Do you agree or disagree with the following statement: Zoos play no useful role in society. Why or why not?

SCORING

Your essay will be rated by two judges and given a score of 0 to 5.

A score of 5 is given to an essay that effectively answers the question, takes and supports a position, demonstrates ability to write in an organized format, includes supporting details, displays good use of English with appropriate word choice.

A score of 4 is given to an essay that addresses all of the above points, but less effectively, with minimum errors.

A score of 3: addresses the above points but with some errors that sometimes hide clarity of meaning.

A score of 2: reveals inadequate organization, lack of supporting details, incorrect word choice, structure or usage errors.

A score of 1: demonstrates serious disorganization, little appropriate detail, serious structure or usage errors, serious lack of focus.

A score of 0: nothing was written, the question was just copied, another language other than English was used.

This scoring information was summarized from the Writing Scoring guide in the official TOEFL Bulletin. Please refer to the bulletin for more complete information on the scoring of the written essay. This information is also available on-line.

Listening Comprehension

Focus on Meaning

Inflection of Voice and Implied Information

Similar or Alike Sounding Words

Opposite Structures

It is quite difficult to improve listening (and reading) skills in a short time. This is an ability that takes years to develop and also takes a long time to improve. That's why this program does not focus on the **Listening Comprehension** section of the TOEFL—it is more focused on the Structure and Written section because it's easier (and more time efficient) to improve this area.

To improve your listening skills, you must *listen*. Try to expose yourself to as much spoken English as possible. Watch TV, see movies, listen to audio recordings. While this program alone may not really be able to improve your listening skills, we can at least try to improve your score by improving your *ability to take the Listening section*.

TIPS and STRATEGIES

PART A—SHORT CONVERSATIONS

In this section of the test you hear a short conversation between **two speakers**, usually a man and a woman to make their voices easily distinguishable. Then, a third speaker asks a question based on this conversation.

Remember, **the question is almost always based on what the second speaker said**. Keeping this in mind, you should anticipate what the question will be before you hear it. This will help you answer quickly and efficiently. To help you do this, don't waste any time—try to get a quick peek at the answer choices before you hear the next conversation, giving you an idea of what the conversation will be about before you hear it.

PARTS B & C—LONGER TALKS

For many, these sections are more difficult because they require that you **understand and remember** more information. Try this: instead of just hearing the conversation, *try to see it*. That's right, use your imagination to picture the conversation taking place. This will help you recall details from your memory.

GENERAL STRATEGY

Always concentrate on the **meaning** of words. Never choose an answer because it repeated a word or phrase that you heard. In fact, choosing an answer that repeats words from the conversation is a poor strategy because the *correct answer usually uses different words*. Again, concentrate on the **meaning** of words, not on the actual words.

Most of the incorrect answers have been designed to sound correct in some way. That makes it hard to eliminate obviously incorrect answers. Wrong answers are **disguised** to seem correct by repeating words you heard or using words that *sound* like words you heard.

Sometimes an incorrect answer will sound perfect but actually have an *opposite meaning*. All of these traps can be avoided with practice (we'll review examples of each one).

Also, pay close attention to the **inflection** of the speaker's voice. Often, the way we say something can greatly affect the meaning of what we say. For example, by changing our inflection we can easily express feelings of surprise, sadness, disbelief, happiness, etc. Try to say the following sentence with an inflection of each of the mentioned emotions:

" The day has arrived. "

Be aware of this because you will often be asked about **implied information**. This is information that is not specifically stated, but implied. Often, the implication is expressed through the inflection of the voice.

In addition to these tips, it is important to remain **concentrated**. During this section of the test, if you begin to think about problems at school or weekend plans, it's likely you'll lose the question, and **nothing will be repeated**. If this happens, don't panic! Put a guessing answer (*never* leave blanks) and focus on the next question. You might miss one question but don't allow a quick loss of concentration cause you to miss several questions by trying to save the one that's lost. *Let it go and refocus.*

Also, remember that ETS tends to write "politically correct" testing material. You can often eliminate an answer that appears in any way controversial or offensive; such language is rarely used in correct answer choices.

The exercises that follow will help you avoid some of the wrong answer choices that have been designed to sound correct. You'll be working with words that sound similar or the same, but have different meanings, and confusing "opposite structures". Remember that meaning and inflection are important.

You'll also find frequent idiomatic expressions in the Listening section—study the Appendix D for practice (or a more complete book of idiomatic expressions if this seems to be a problem for you.)

Before you work through the exercises, take a close look at the following **example question** that demonstrates clearly the kinds of wrong answers we want to eliminate. We will see how the right answer often sounds different from the conversation we heard. The same "traps" are found in all of the Listening sections. The right answer might sound wrong—the wrong answers, right.

You Hear:

Man: Did you finish this week's reading assignment?

Woman: I finished it, but I couldn't make heads or tails of it.

Question: What does the woman mean?

In your test book you read:

A) She can barely understand any of the material.

B) She finished the tale ahead of schedule.

C) She thought the book was stupid and an insult to her intelligence.

D) She preferred not to accept the bet.

Now let's examine each of the four answers. Notice how the wrong answers are designed in various ways to seem correct—the correct answer is designed to seem incorrect.

Choice (A) is the **correct choice**, but notice how it uses an **"opposite structure"**. You heard, "...I couldn't..." and the correct answer uses "She can barely..." The *meaning* is the same although what you heard uses a negative structure while the answer choice uses an affirmative structure with a negative word.

Choice (B) is designed to sound correct because of **similar and alike** sounding words. The word "finished" is repeated, "tale" sounds like "tails" and "ahead" sounds like "heads".

Choice (C) should be eliminated because it is a bit **aggressive**. It is rare to find a correct answer that sounds so offensive. It would be more common to find something like "She didn't agree completely with the book's proposal". The "...stupid..." and "...insult to her intelligence..." in this answer choice is somewhat offensive.

Choice (D) mixes up the meaning of an **idiomatic expression**. "...heads or tails..." usually refers to flipping a coin but "...not making heads or tails..." can also mean that something is too difficult to understand. If you pay attention to the speaker's intonation you should understand that the speaker was not referring to making a bet. Also avoid choosing answers based on the literal meaning of the words, rather than the real implication, of an idiomatic expression.

EXERCISE L-1 (Similar Sounds)

Directions: You will hear 20 words spoken by your teacher (or study partner). Try to choose the one you heard and mark it with an (X).

1. _____ (A) pal
   _____ (B) pill

2. _____ (A) sheet
   _____ (B) sheep

3. _____ (A) bins
   _____ (B) beans

4. _____ (A) backs
   _____ (B) box

5. _____ (A) duck
   _____ (B) dock

6. _____ (A) rest
   _____ (B) wrist

7. _____ (A) chair
   _____ (B) Cher

8. _____ (A) cream
   _____ (B) scream

9. _____ (A) lung
   _____ (B) long

10. _____ (A) pen
    _____ (B) pan

11. _____ (A) chicks
    _____ (B) checks

12. _____ (A) worm
    _____ (B) warm

13. _____ (A) high
    _____ (B) hay

14. _____ (A) last
    _____ (B) lost

15. _____ (A) 60
    _____ (B) 16

16. _____ (A) hitting
    _____ (B) heating

17. _____ (A) fill
    _____ (B) fell

18. _____ (A) tray
    _____ (B) try

19. _____ (A) could
    _____ (B) couldn't

20. _____ (A) four
    _____ (B) floor

EXERCISE L-2 (Alike Sounds)

Directions: Complete the following sentences by choosing (**A**) or (**B**). Here, the sounds are the same, but the meanings are different.

_____ 1. That was quite a _____.
(A) feet   (B) feat

_____ 2. Read me the _____.
(A) tale   (B) tail

_____ 3. The judge tries to be _____.
(A) fare   (B) fair

_____ 4. We'll go in the _____.
(A) mourning   (B) morning

_____ 5. Your argument is _____.
(A) week   (B) weak

_____ 6. He _____ to Nicaragua.
(A) flew   (B) flu

_____ 7. The fast chef cooks with _____.
         (A) time   (B) thyme

_____ 8. The farmer's wife is _____ a dress.
         (A) sowing   (B) sewing

_____ 9. We will fly over the _____.
         (A) plane   (B) plain

_____ 10. She _____ me clean my room.
         (A) maid   (B) made

_____ 11. I hit the pitch _____ left field.
         (A) through   (B) threw

_____ 12. What beautiful _____ of flowers!
         (A) rose   (B) rows

_____ 13. The broken glass caused my _____.
         (A) pain   (B) pane

_____ 14. You'll be _____ for losing the book.
         (A) find   (B) fined

_____ 15. Try to _____ correctly.
         (A) right   (B) write

EXERCISE L-3 (Opposite Structures)

Directions: Choose the answer that *means* the same (although it uses an opposite structure or different words) as the one you hear. Circle (**A**) or (**B**). Pay attention to *implied* information.

1.   You Hear: Jim always goes to church on Sunday.

       (A) Jim hardly attends church on Sunday.
       (B) Jim never misses church on Sunday.

2.   You Hear: I have a hard time with algebra.

       (A) I don't have time for my algebra homework.
       (B) I can't easily understand algebra.

3.   You Hear: He's not crazy about football.

       (A) He's a football fanatic.
       (B) He likes other things more than football.

4.   You Hear: I can't stand to ride a bus that long.

       (A) I prefer to ride the bus for shorter periods of time.
       (B) I love to take long bus rides.

5.   You Hear: I never drink anything except diet soft drinks.

       (A) I always drink normal soft drinks.
       (B) I only drink diet soft drinks.

6.   You Hear: I prefer industrial music to rap.

(A) I think rap is better than industrial music.
(B) I don't like rap better than industrial.

7.   You Hear: The new *Star Wars* movie doesn't compare to the original.

(A) The original is better.
(B) The new one is just as good.

8.   You Hear: A laser printer produces better results than an ink jet.

(A) The ink jet isn't as good as the laser.
(B) The laser is just as good as the ink jet.

9.   You Hear: I don't like contemporary designs as much as antiques.

(A) I like antiques better than contemporary designs.
(B) I prefer contemporary designs to antiques.

10.   You Hear: I always take the subway home from work.

(A) I never drive home from work.
(B) I sometimes skip the subway ride.

11.   You Hear: I have a poor understanding of grammatical rules.

(A) I understand perfectly the grammatical rules.
(B) I'm not an expert in grammatical rules.

12.   You Hear: The little boy loves nothing more than hot-
       dogs.

       (A) The little boy is crazy about hotdogs.
       (B) The little boy might prefer hamburgers.

13.   You Hear: There is a 90% chance of rain tonight.

       (A) Rain tonight is doubtful.
       (B) You can plan on rain tonight.

14.   You Hear: Paris is somewhat more populated than
       Niece.

       (A) Niece is more populated than Paris.
       (B) Paris has more people than Niece.

15.   You Hear: The registration deadline is tomorrow.

       (A) You could not register after yesterday.
       (B) You can't register after tomorrow.

Reading Comprehension & Vocabulary

Question Types

Strategic Tips

This is probably the **least time efficient** area of the test to try preparing for. It is especially difficult to try and improve one's vocabulary in a short time—even if you study good lists with thousands of words, there's no guarantee that any of these words will be tested when you take the TOEFL. Likewise, general reading skills can't really be improved quickly.

To improve your reading skills—**you must read**. As you prepare for the TOEFL, set up a reading schedule. Try to read an hour or two every day. Obviously, a library with books in English would be very useful. **Read a variety of materials**: short passages from textbooks, magazines, encyclopedias, newspapers, etc. List especially difficult words to check later in the dictionary.

Just as in the Listening section of this book, we'll concentrate here on **strategies**—test-taking skills that help you understand how to answer as many correct answers as possible. As in all sections of the test, it is important here to be familiar with the directions (so you don't waste any time reading them when you take the test). Also, make sure you understand the format of the test—what types of questions you can expect to find. We'll discuss these in detail and offer some strategic advice on how to answer each question type.

In the Institutional TOEFL format (ITP), only multiple choice questions are included. We will review the seven types of questions included on the ITP. Make sure you review these. Learn to recognize them so that you can answer them in the best order. (On the iBT, we have a greater variety of question formats, but the types of questions are similar.)

Many students prefer to read the passage completely before answering any questions. But remember: **you won't get any points for careful reading—only for correct answers!** Don't study the passage—get to the questions with as much time as possible. The total time on ITP is 55 mins.

Don't even begin reading the passage until you've reviewed the questions first. Your focus should be on the **questions**, not on memorizing the passage which contains a lot of useless information. With practice you'll get better at "pulling out" the answers you need without reading word for word. You'll learn to **skim for key words** that help you quickly find the answers.

Time is very important in this section—that's why we want to be as familiar as possible with the types of questions, the directions, and the general format. Remember, you can answer the questions in any order, so **answer easy questions first**. If you do run out of time before you answer the questions, don't panic. Instead, try the **Running out of Time Strategy** found after the explanations of question types that follows.

QUESTION TYPES

1. MAIN IDEA QUESTIONS

You will often find this question **first** but you want to answer it **last**. This will be a very general question. For example:

What is the main topic of the passage?

If you answer the other questions first, you will gather more information about the topic and main idea which will help you correctly answer this type of question.

2. VOCABULARY-IN-CONTEXT QUESTIONS

Vocabulary skills are tested by asking questions about words within the reading passage. Given that many words in English have multiple meanings, we have to pay attention to the context in which the words are used. Remember, **all of the answer choices will fit correctly** grammatically if substituted. It's still a case of "you know the word or you don't know it" usually. Of course, there is some **strategy** that can be used to improve your chances of getting a vocabulary-in-context question correct.

Be able to recognize this type of question. It will be worded like this example:

The word "catastrophic" in line 12 is closest in meaning to... (followed by 4 answer choices).

Before you review the answer choices, go to line 12 and try to replace the word with another word or phrase that will retain the original meaning of the sentence. This will help you eliminate words that **sound** right, but have different meanings. Compare your substituted word with the answer choices.

3. KEY WORD QUESTIONS

Obviously, these are questions that are based on key words and are sometimes the easiest to answer. A key word question will be worded like this example:

According to the passage, photosynthesis occurs primarily as a result of...

Can you **identify the key word**? It is, of course, *photosynthesis*. Now, go back to the passage and look for this word. Read the sentence before the one with the key word and the sentence in which it appears. You should find the answer to your question, but if not, quickly **skim** to see if the key word appears again. If the key word appears frequently, maybe you've chosen the wrong word, or maybe the question is really a more general one—examine the question again.

4. REFERENCE QUESTIONS

Reference questions ask you to identify what a noun, pronoun, or phrase refers to. A reference question will be worded like this example:

In line 4, *they* **refers to…** (followed by 4 answer choices).

The best strategy here is **substitution**. Try substituting the word in question with your answer choices until you find the one that doesn't change the meaning of the sentence. Read the sentence in which the word in question appears as well as the sentence before. Remember, the reference is not always found with the closest words.

Read the following sentence and try to pick the correct reference from the answer choices that follow.

1. Recently, scientists questioned whether Pluto actually met
2. the criteria of being classified as a planet. Some even sug-
3. gested that <u>it</u> be deleted from the list of planets in our…

in line 3, *it* **refers to…**

> (A) criterion
> (B) the list
> (C) planet
> (D) Pluto

5. NEGATIVE QUESTIONS

These questions, which include words such as *except, not,* or *least likely,* ask you to identify what is **not mentioned** in the passage, A negative question will be worded like this example:

None of the animals in the zoo were infected with the dis-ease EXCEPT… (followed by 4 choices).

Find the key word "animals", then go to the passage where animals are mentioned and begin **eliminating answers**. When you've eliminated 3 choices, you're left with the correct answer.

6. BEFORE & AFTER QUESTIONS

These are hypothetical questions that ask you to put lines logically within a text or to identify what might have been written immediately before or after a passage. A before and after question will be worded like this example:

The paragraph following this passage will most likely discuss what?... (followed by 4 choices).

Here, use common sense—concentrate on the "cause and effect" or what was or will be a logical chain of events. For **"before" questions**, make sure your answer choice includes the same main subject. For **"after" questions**, concentrate on the final two sentences. In these last sentences you should find a quick summary of what was said with clues as to where the next paragraph will begin.

7. INFERENCE QUESTIONS

In inference questions you must literally **"read between the lines"**. These questions, similar to those in Listening Comprehension, will ask questions about information that is implied but not specifically stated. An inference question will be worded like this example:

It can be inferred from the passage that... (followed by 4 answer choices).

These are quite similar to main idea questions—**you'll need a general idea about the complete passage** to answer them correctly. These tend to be difficult and should be saved, along with main idea questions, until all other questions have been considered and answered. Answering the other questions will help you gather information to make logical, general inferences.

RUNNING OUT OF TIME STRATEGY

If the time has run down to **three minutes**, you should have no more than one unread passage. First, answer any questions with line numbers—these could include "vocabulary in context" or "reference" questions. Then try to skim quickly through the passage and answer "key word" questions. By now, you should have a general idea of the passage and might be able to answer the "main idea" question (usually the first one) and maybe a "negative fact" or "inference" question. If you don't have time to study the more difficult types of questions, try to eliminate answers and guess with the answer that sounds more logical. With only **5 seconds** left, put a guessing letter for answers you could not study more carefully—never leave a blank.

Again, being familiar with the most common **types of questions** and how to answer them is your best strategy in this section. Always go to the questions **before reading** the passage. Answer the **easiest questions first**. Be careful with **time**.

Try to get **reading practice**—for extra practice see if you can formulate questions that are like the various types we've just seen. This will help you think like the people who actually write the questions. You might even try to write out some incorrect answers.

For most students, the Reading section will be their best. Remember, if you're a little weak in the Listening Comprehension or Structure and Written Expression sections—this is your opportunity to pull up your overall score.

APPENDICES

APPENDIX A

IRREGULAR VERBS

SIMPLE	PAST	PAST PARTICI-PLE
be	was, were	been
become	became	become
begin	began	begun
bend	bent	bent
bite	bit	bitten
blow	blew	blown
break	broke	broken
bring	brought	brought
broadcast	broadcast	broadcast
build	built	built
buy	bought	bought
catch	caught	caught
come	came	come
cost	cost	cost
cut	cut	cut
dig	dug	dug
do	did	done
draw	drew	drawn
drink	drank	drunk
drive	drove	driven
eat	ate	eaten
fall	fell	fallen
feed	fed	fed
feel	felt	felt
fight	fought	fought
find	found	found
fit	fit	fit
fly	flew	flown

forget	forgot	forgotten
forgive	forgave	forgiven
freeze	froze	frozen
get	got	gotten
give	gave	given
go	went	gone
grow	grew	grown
hang	hung	hung
have	had	had
hear	heard	heard
hide	hid	hidden
hit	hit	hit
hold	held	held
hurt	hurt	hurt
keep	kept	kept
know	knew	known
lay	laid	laid
lead	led	led
leave	left	left
lend	lent	lent
let	let	let
lie	lay	lain
light	lit (lighted)	lit (lighted)
lose	lost	lost
make	made	made
mean	meant	meant
meet	met	met
pay	paid	paid
put	put	put
quit	quit	quit
read	read	read
ride	rode	ridden
ring	rang	rung
rise	rose	risen
run	ran	run
say	said	said

see	saw	seen
sell	sold	sold
send	sent	sent
set	set	set
shake	shook	shaken
shoot	shot	shot
shut	shut	shut
sing	sang	sung
sit	sat	sat
sleep	slept	slept
slide	slid	slid
speak	spoke	spoken
spend	spent	spent
spread	spread	spread
stand	stood	stood
steal	stole	stolen
stick	stuck	stuck
strike	struck	struck
swear	swore	sworn
sweep	swept	swept
swing	swung	swung
swim	swam	swum
take	took	taken
teach	taught	taught
tear	tore	torn
tell	told	told
think	thought	thought
throw	threw	thrown
understand	understood	understood
upset	upset	upset
wake	woke	waked (woken)
wear	wore	worn
win	won	won
withdraw	withdrew	withdrawn
write	wrote	written

POP QUIZ

Can you work through the list and give a Hindi translation of each of the verbs?

APPENDIX B

PHRASAL VERBS
(A Mini Dictionary of Common Clusters)

Phrasal verbs are idiomatic combinations of verbs and other parts of speech. Many are obvious in meaning—they're easily formed and understood. Others are more difficult—especially multiple forms using the same verb with varying meaning. Those are the focus of the following listing.

A

Act as—to play the role of
Act for—to represent someone
Act up—to misbehave or to become painful or problematic
Act up to—to live up to (expectations)
Act upon—to take action regarding

Add in—to put something in the middle
Add on—to put something extra at the end, to expand one's home
Add to—to increase, to make a sum
Add together—to total all parts
Add up—to make a total of numbers, or to make sense
Add up to—to amount to

Allow for—to take into consideration, to provide
Allow in—to permit to enter

Allow to—to permit an action
Allow up—to release from bed (medical conditions)

Answer back—to respond to someone in a rude manner
Answer for—to account for, to answer in the place of someone else, to take the responsibility for
Answer to—to be called a name, to obey, to report to someone
Answer up—to respond clearly, without fear

Appear at—to arrive or perform at a certain place, to face a court of law
Appear before—to arrive before a certain time, to face a court of law
Appear for—to act as a lawyer for someone in a court of law
Appear in—to suddenly be seen, to perform in, to be published in
Appear on—to be displayed on
Appear under—to perform using a name

Ask about—to request information
Ask after—to inquire about someone's health
Ask back—to have back, to invite to return
Ask for—to request, to invite trouble
Ask in (or up)—to invite someone in your home
Ask of—to request, to expect from
Ask out—to invite on a date
Ask over—to invite a visit
Ask to—to request help

B

Back away—to move away in fear
Back down—to accept defeat in an argument
Back into—to enter or to hit something when driving

Back off—to retreat from
Back out—to get out of a commitment
Back up—to support, to go backwards

NOTE: The number of phrasal verbs that can be formed with the verb **"to be"** is too great to address in the context of this list. Please consult a dictionary of phrasal verbs if you need to review this.

Break away—to escape, to come apart
Break down—to be defeated, to stop working (machines), to reduce or destroy
Break even—to show no gain and no loss
Break in—to enter by force, to interrupt, to wear new shoes for the first time
Break into—to divide into parts, to enter by force
Break loose—to escape, to become out of control
Break off—to come apart, to end a relationship
Break open—to open by force
Break out—to unwrap or open, to have an outbreak (medical)
Break up—to divide or destroy, to end a relationship

Bring about—to cause to happen
Bring along—to carry with
Bring around—to persuade someone to change an opinion
Bring back—to take something back to its original place
Bring down—to defeat, to reduce (prices)
Bring in—to bring indoors, to gather (crops)
Bring on—to cause to appear
Bring out—to produce, to cause to be noticed

C

Call away—to cause a departure (usually for business purposes)
Call back—to ask someone to return, to return a telephone call
Call for—to need or deserve, to demand something, to arrive to collect
Call in—to ask someone to attend, to pay a short visit (ships)
Call off—to cancel, to cause to keep away (usually an animal)
Call on (upon)—to visit, on business or socially
Call out—to shout
Call over—to ask someone to come to where you are
Call up—to give someone a telephone call, to remember

Carry away—to take away, to excite or persuade
Carry forward—to move a figure to the next page (business)
Carry off—to succeed, to remove (usually by force)
Carry on—to take something with you (usually in an airplane), to continue in spite of difficulties
Carry over—to move to a later date, to move a figure to the next page (business)
Carry through—to help someone live through danger, to lift
Carry with—to take with you, to persuade someone to support you

Catch it—to be reprimanded
Catch on—to become popular, to understand
Catch up—to reach someone who is ahead, to have a detailed conversation after a long absence

Chop down—to make fall (usually a tree)
Chop off—to cut off, to remove with an axe
Chop up—to cut into smaller pieces

Come about—to happen

Come across—to travel a short distance, to find, to be understood

Come across as—to seem to be

Come after—to follow, to chase

Come along—to arrive with someone, to pass, to arrive by chance

Come apart—to break into parts

Come between—to happen between, to get in the way, to interrupt

Come by—to obtain or receive

Come clean—to admit

Come down—to move to a lower level, to get sick, to reduce, to pass along through family generations

Come forward—to move to the front, to offer your help

Come next—to follow

Come out—to move outside, to be removed

Come through—to pass through something, to do what is hoped for, to survive in spite of difficulty

Come to—to reach a point, to regain consciousness, to move near

Come up—to create an idea, to rise

D

Do about—to take action about something

Do badly—to be in poor health, to be unsuccessful

Do for—to serve the purpose of

Do good—to help people, to improve

Do in—to murder, to ruin

Do over—to repeat, to improve the appearance of something

Do up—to make oneself more attractive, to wrap or tie in an arrangement

Do with—to be satisfied with, to control, to deal with
Do without—to survive without something you need

Drive at—to suggest something
Drive away—to work hard at something, to leave in a vehicle
Drive back—to force backwards
Drive crazy (or mad)—to annoy, to cause someone to go mad
Drive home—to make a point understood, to travel to one's home
Drive in—to teach with force, to force into position with a hammer
Drive off—to make go away, to cause to go back
Drive out—to make someone or something move away

Drop in—to arrive informally for a visit (usually unannounced)
Drop it—to stop doing something or talking about something
Drop off—to leave someone somewhere, to become worse, to fall asleep.
Drop out—to choose to leave (usually school), to fall out of

E

Eat away—to gradually destroy
Eat into—to use part of, to harm or have a bad effect
Eat out—to eat in a restaurant, or out of the house
Eat up—to use a lot of, to defeat, to hurt emotionally

Enter by—to go into a place using a certain entrance
Enter in—to write something in a record
Enter into—to begin something, to begin to examine or work with, to write in a record
Enter upon (on)—to begin, to take responsibility for (formal)

F

Fall apart—to end in failure, to break into pieces without being forced
Fall back on—to use one's reserved resources or someone's help
Fall behind—to be behind schedule or late in paying money
Fall down—to tumble down (usually a building), to accidentally fall
Fall from—to lose one's high standing ("fall from grace"—to become immoral)
Fall in—to accidentally fall into, to get into formation, to be ruined.
Fall into—to be divided among kinds, to begin a state of being
Fall off—to become worse, to become suddenly lower (geographical or financial)
Fall out—to have a dispute, to tumble out
Fall short—to be left with less than expected

Frighten away (off)—to scare someone into leaving
Frighten into—to force someone with fear to do something
Frighten out of—to prevent someone with fear from doing something

G

Note: The number of phrasal verbs that can be formed with the verbs **"to get"** and **"to go"** is too great to address in the context of this list. Please consult a dictionary of phrasal verbs if you need to review this.

Grow apart—to become separated
Grow away from—to become independent of
Grow back—to return to original length (often with hair)
Grow from—to develop from
Grow in—to develop or increase size in regard to a quality ("grow in number")
Grow into—to become accustomed to, to grow larger so as to fit (for clothing)
Grow on—to gradually like more, to become habit
Grow out—to become larger (in an outward direction)
Grow up—to become more mature, to develop

H

Hang around—to stay near a certain place
Hang back (off)—to hesitate in acting, keep oneself in the background
Hang in—to keep trying in spite of difficulties
Hang on—to depend on something, to wait, to continue holding
Hang out—to spend leisure time at a particular place
Hang over—to threaten or surround with fear or doubt, to be in a state of suffering after drinking too much alcohol
Hang up—to put the telephone receiver down, to be stubborn about something, to delay

Hold back—to control (feelings), to delay
Hold dear—to value highly, to respect
Hold down—to keep food in the stomach, to control, to keep employed ("hold down a job"), keep at a lower level
Hold in—to control (feelings), to keep inward
Hold off—to cause delay

Hold on—to continue in spite of difficulties, to continue holding

Hold out—to last, to stretch forward (your hand)

Hold up—to delay, to rob, to wait for someone

I

Identify by—identify by means of something (or someone) else

Identify oneself—to reveal one's name

Identify with—to feel the same way, to feel sympathy for

J

Join in—to take part

Join in with—to take part with someone (or a group), to share the cost

Join with—to share the feelings of someone

Jump at—to eagerly accept an opportunity

Jump down—to spring downward ("jump down one's throat" means to be angry with)

Jump in—to be eager to participate, to spring into the middle

Jump off—to spring off of something

Jump out of—to leave suddenly ("jump out of one's skin" means to be very afraid)

Jump to—to go quickly to

Jump up—to rise suddenly

K

Keep abreast of—to stay completely informed
Keep after—to find fault, to continuously ask someone to do something, to continue chasing
Keep ahead—to remain in advance of
Keep apart—to maintain separate
Keep away from—to avoid, to keep at a distance from someone
Keep by—to maintain close to
Keep cool—to remain calm, to prevent from becoming warm
Keep from—to avoid, to stop or delay an action
Keep going—to continue an activity
Keep off—to cause to remain at a distance
Keep up—to continue, to keep prices high, to remain the same (usually weather), to maintain good condition

Kick back—to fire backwards (an engine), to keep a portion of a financial profit
Kick down—to make fall by kicking
Kick in—to damage by kicking, to add a share of money
Kick out—to make someone leave a place, to push outside with the foot
Kick up—to make noise or trouble

Knock down—to make fall by hitting, to destroy a building, to reduce the price
Knock off—to reduce the price, to stop working, to murder, to stop something that annoys someone
Knock on—to strike a hard object
Knock out—to hit someone and force a loss of consciousness, to cause to go to sleep (with medication), to remove with a hit
Knock over—to make something fall by hitting it, to easily defeat

Know about—to be informed about something
Know as—to be called by a name
Know best—to be the best judge
Know better—to have more sense
Know of—to have knowledge about

L

Lay away—to save for a customer to purchase
Lay before—to place in front of, to offer before an official government body
Lay down—to state firmly, to risk money
Lay low—to hide (usually from authorities)
Lay off—to rest, to stop doing something, to end employment
Lay out—to spread for use or viewing, to introduce a plan
Lay over—to make an overnight stop during a trip

Leave behind—to go away without talking
Leave in—to allow to remain inside or a part of
Leave out—to fail to include on a list, to fail to consider, to place something for someone, to ignore
Leave with—to give someone a responsibility, to remain in the care of someone

Let alone—to not have anything to do with, to not mention, to not bother
Let by—to allow to pass without comment
Let down—to fail to keep a promise, to lower
Let in—to admit, to allow to enter a place
Let loose—to allow freedom
Let off—to allow to leave, to excuse from punishment
Let on—to tell a secret, to pretend

Live down—to cause people to forget
Live for—to wish for, to have as a reason for living
Live off—to find sufficient income, to live at the cost of someone else
Live through—to remain alive in spite of difficulty, to experience
Live up—to enjoy life
Live up to—to behave in a manner worthy of

Look ahead—to think about the future, to see in front
Look alike—to have the same appearance
Look back—to think about the past, to see behind
Look down on—to have a poor opinion of someone
Look forward to—to expect and wait for
Look out—to be cautious, to have a view of
Look up to—to respect or to admire

M

Make away with—to steal or destroy
Make certain—to be sure of the truth
Make good—to repay a debt, to live a successful life
Make light of—to make something seem less serious than it really is
Make out—to write, to see clearly, to understand, to reach an answer, to claim, to kiss passionately
Make over—to change the appearance of something or someone, to remake
Make up—to invent a story, to apply cosmetics to the face, to be part of, to take an exam outside of the normal schedule
Make up for—to repay, provide a balance for

Move away—to live somewhere else, to change one's opinion

Move forward—to advance or improve, to go ahead
Move in—to take control or to attack, to assume a place of residence
Move in on—to share a place without permission, to surround and attack
Move over—to yield one's position, to move to another place

N

Name after—to give someone the name of someone else
Name as—to give a title to someone
Note down—to record in writing
Note for—to be famous because of

O

Open into—to provide a view of
Open out—to spread or become wide open
Open up—to bring within reach (usually a possibility), to open for business, to speak more freely

P

Pass by—to overlook or disregard, to pass without pleasure (usually life), to grow later (time), to move past
Pass down—to send from person to person, to give to younger family members (often clothing)

Pass off—to make someone accept by deceit, to succeed in pretending to be something (or someone)
Pass up—to fail to take advantage of an opportunity, to give to someone on a higher level

Pick apart—to find fault in, to separate the pieces of
Pick at—to play with instead of eating food, to make fun of
Pick from—to choose from a group, to remove
Pick out—to recognize in a crowd, to play a musical melody by ear, to choose
Pick up—to collect, to meet romantically, to give someone a ride, to lift, to tidy a room, to obtain cheaply, to improve (business)

Play along—to pretend to agree with, to keep waiting for an answer
Play back—to hear a recording again
Play out—to perform, to mark the end of, to finish playing a game
Play safe—to avoid risk and possibility of failure

Pull aside—to take one away for a private conversation
Pull for—to cheer for (usually a sports team)
Pull off—to succeed in spite of difficulty, to drive to the side of the road, to remove by force
Pull out—to move away, to get of a commitment
Pull over—to drive to the side of the road
Pull through—to survive in spite of difficulty, to make pass through
Pull together—to work together on a common goal, to improve
Pull up—to come to a stop, to lift, to correct, or to improve

Put across—to make understood, to place in a position crossing something
Put ahead—to move a clock forward, to advance

Put away—to store in a box or space, to eat a lot of food, to save money, to stop thinking about

Put back—to return, to regain weight, to cost money, to delay, to move a clock backwards

Put behind—to delay, to end a difficult situation

Put down—to record in writing, to criticize, to eat a lot of food, to lower, to pay part of a price

Put off—to delay, to discourage

Put up—to increase in cost, to provide funds, to provide overnight accommodation, to take something out of use

Put up with—to tolerate

R

Rest against—to lean on for support

Rest in—to exist because of, to lie in comfort, sleep, or death ("rest in peace")

Rest on (upon)—to cause to lie safely or comfortably in sleep or death, to cause to touch or reach, to depend on

Rest up—to have a complete rest after an illness, to catch up on sleep

Run about—to use a vehicle for driving around, to run without direction

Run across—to pass over a space, to find or meet someone or something by chance

Run after—to chase, to flirt with, to attempt to achieve something

Run against—to compete with in an election

Run amuck—to behave out of control

Run away—to escape, to flow away, to leave by running

Run behind—to be behind schedule

Run down—to knock down and damage, to find by searching, to flow downward, to lose power

Run in—to enter quickly, to flow into, to arrest (by police)
Run through—to flow through something, to be part of, to send (money) fast, to read quickly, to repeat for practice
Run up—to raise (a flag), to allow to increase, to increase the price of

S

See about—to deal with or to attend, to make arrangements
See after—to take care of or to take responsibility for
See ahead—to think about, to plan for, to see in the distance
See around—to see or meet someone regularly
See fit—to decide that it is correct to do something
See in—to show into a room or building, to have a reason for liking
See over—to look around, to have sight over the top of something
See through—to work until finished, to look through something invisible

Set ahead—to move the hour of a clock to a later time, to change an event to an earlier date
Set apart—to place separately, to be or feel differently from others
Set aside—to stop paying attention to (feelings), to discontinue, to place on one side
Set before—to offer for consideration or approval, to place in front of
Set beside—to place next to, to compare
Set in—to begin and seem likely to continue (weather and medical conditions), to put in something (such as a frame), to print with a certain kind of type, to provide with a setting in a particular place (such as a book)
Set off— to begin a trip, to start happening

Set out—to begin a profession, to begin a trip, to spread for use, to make known, to start an activity, to plant
Set right—to correct, to make someone feel better (with medicine)
Set up—to start, to put in a certain position, to establish, to cause to receive the blame

Show around—to take a tour of a place
Show for—to have as a result of
Show off (out)—to show pride in, to behave with a sense of self-importance, to accentuate the best qualities
Show up—to arrive, to accentuate, to lead upstairs, to make to look foolish, to win a competition

Sleep around—to have sexual relations with many people
Sleep in—to sleep late
Sleep over—to stay overnight at someone's home
Sleep through—to remain sleeping through an event (such as bad weather)

Stand aside—to take no action, to move to one side
Stand back—to maintain one's distance, to refuse to take part in
Stand between—to try to prevent an action, to be in a position between two other things or people
Stand by—to be loyal to someone, to be ready for action, to be near something
Stand for—to support, to represent, to believe in, to accept
Stand out—to be noticeable, to be of better quality
Stand up for—to demand, to support

T

Take after—to look like, to begin to chase, to swallow after a certain point (medicine)

Take apart—to separate into parts, to severely criticize

Take as—to understand or assume to be as

Take down—to record in writing, to remove from a higher position, to disassemble

Take off—to remove, to leave or go away, to rise from the ground (airplane), to reduce weight

Take on—to accept work, to employ, to accept as an opponent, to begin to show a quality, to become popular

Take out—to remove, to remove a stain, to take food outside a restaurant, to lead or carry outside

Take over—to win control of, to accept responsibility for

Talk about—to gossip about, to consider an idea, to have a conversation about

Talk back—to reply (often rudely)

Talk down—to speak to as if another person is less important, to criticize

Talk into—to persuade into doing something, to direct the voice into something (a telephone)

Talk out (over)—to consider completely, to settle by talking

Talk out of—to persuade someone against doing something

Throw away—to get rid of, to fail, to take advantage of

Throw back—to delay the advance of, to return by throwing

Throw down—to defeat or destroy, to direct with force to the ground

Throw in—to add as a gift, to stop attempting, to include or add, to direct with force into something

Throw off—to surprise ("throw off guard"), to release heat or smell, to remove quickly (clothing)

Throw open—to open quickly, to declare free to enter

Turn around—to improve after failing, to change one's opinion, to change a person's version of a story, to move the other way

Turn away—to refuse entry, to refuse, to move in a direction away from

Turn back—to stop moving forward, to cause to go backwards, to turn to a previous page in a book

Turn down—to fold backwards (the sheets of a bed), to refuse to accept

Turn in—to drive into a place, to give something back after use, to present (homework), to go to bed

Turn into—to change and cause to become something or someone else

Turn loose—to give someone freedom to act as he wishes, to free

Turn off—to stop with a control (water), to drive in a different direction, to cease to like

Turn on—to start with a control (water), to attack someone (a dog), to be attracted to

Turn out—to stop with a switch (the lights), to turn inside out, to result, to gather in large numbers

Turn over—to start an engine, to trade a sum of money, to leave one's place of employment

Turn to—to change into, to go for help, to direct one's attention to

Turn up—to happen, to arrive unexpectedly, to find by chance, to increase the volume

W

Wait at—to stay in a place expecting something or someone
Wait for—to expect something or to stay in a place expecting something or someone
Wait on—to continue waiting, to attend to (a waiter in a restaurant)
Wait out—to wait for something to be over with (usually a storm)
Wait up—to delay going to bed until someone arrives, to delay to wait for another person

Walk away from—to leave unhurt (a crash), to defeat
Walk in—to be able to secure a job easily, to enter without permission or appointment
Walk off—to leave suddenly, to reduce by walking (weight, pain, problem)
Walk on—to take a small role in a play, to be inconsiderate of
Walk out—to leave in opposition, to refuse to work in protest, to go outside
Walk out on—to desert someone, to fail to fulfil an agreement

Work at—to have one's job at a particular place, to put effort into something
Work for—to be employed by someone, to do a job in order to earn
Work in—to enter gradually, to be able to include in a written work
Work loose—to cause to become loose
Work off—to cause to end by working, to pay a debt with work instead of money, to cause with movement to become loose

Work out—to calculate, to force loose with movement, to invent or develop, to understand, to find an answer to, to exercise

Work up to—to excite and reach a state, to begin to reach a point, to prepare to say something, to gradually get near

Work with—to have the company and help of, to perform work with the aid of something, to have a cooperative spirit

APPENDIX C

VERBS USED WITH GERUNDS OR INFINITIVES

With most verbs it is OK to use a gerund or an infinitive as a compliment: *I like swimming* is the same as *I like to swim*. However, there are few verbs that should only be used with a gerund or only with an infinitive. Those are included here.

VERBS USED WITH A GERUND

admit, anticipate, appreciate, avoid, complete, consider, delay, deny, discuss, dislike, enjoy, finish, keep, mention, miss, postpone, practice, quit, recall, recommend, regret, resent, resist, risk, stop, suggest, tolerate, understand

VERBS USED WITH AN INFINITIVE

afford, agree, appear, arrange, ask, beg, care, claim, consent, dare, decide, demand, deserve, encourage, expect, fail, forget, hesitate, hope, instruct, intend, learn, manage, mean, need, offer, order, permit, plan, prepare, pretend, promise, refuse, remind, require, seem, struggle, tend, threaten, volunteer, wait, want, wish

APPENDIX D

100 COMMON IDIOMATIC EXPRESSIONS

Here, we include a glossary of 100 common idioms. These are often heard in the Listening Comprehension section of the TOEFL. Some of them are quite similar to phrasal verbs. Some of them function as part of longer expressions. This is only a sample of the hundreds of idioms that exist in American English. Remember, on the TOEFL you might be tricked by idioms when answer choices refer to their literal, rather than implied, meaning.

1. **all thumbs**—to be clumsy, not coordinated, especially with the hands

2. **ball of fire**—describes a person who has a lot of energy and ambition

3. **be on target**—to be exactly right in one's analysis of something

4. **be tied up**—to be very busy

5. **beat to the draw**—to win a race

6. **blow the whistle**—to reveal secret information

7. **blow one's own horn**—to promote oneself, to call attention to one's skills

8. **butt in**—to interrupt

9. **call the shots**—to be in charge, to give commands

10. **can of worms**—a complex problem, a whole new set of complications

11. **catch one's eye**—to attract one's attention

12. **clown around**—to be silly, to not be serious

13. **come out of one's shell**—to stop being shy and become more extraverted

14. **cry over spilled milk**—to be upset over something that has happened and can't be undone

15. **down in the dumps**—feeling low, in a bad mood or depressed

16. **eager beaver**—a person who is enthusiastic and hardworking

17. **end of one's rope**—the position whereby a person can no longer cope or try

18. **fed up with**—tired of dealing with—annoyed

19. **flat broke**—having no money

20. **get a word in edgewise**—successfully making a comment to a person who is controlling the conversation

21. **get off the ground**—to successfully begin, such as a business

22.   **get one's goat**—to get on one's nerves, to make very angry

23.   **get the message**—understand a subtle hint, understand what is meant

24.   **get through one's head**—to convince

25.   **give a hand**—to applaud or to help someone

26.   **give a hard time**—to make problems for someone

27.   **green thumb**—the ability to grow plants well, especially flowers

28.   **hang up**—an unexpected delay, an unnatural feeling about a normal life occurrence, to break a phone line

29.   **hard act to follow**—a great performance that will be hard to compete with

30.   **have a hand in**—to be involved in

31.   **have well in hand**—to have perfectly under control

32.   **head over heels**—to be in love with

33.   **heads or tails**—describes the action of flipping a coin or being completely ignorant of ("…can't make heads or tails of…")

34.   **hit the jackpot**—to be extremely lucky, to win

35.   **hit the nail on the head**—to get something exactly right, to completely understand

36. **horse of another color**—something completely different from something else

37. **hot under the collar**—really angry, agitated

38. **in a bind**—with a real problem or conflict

39. **in a stew**—in a state of anger

40. **in one's right mind**—to be sane

41. **in the doghouse**—in big trouble with someone

42. **jump on the bandwagon**—join a larger group of people by sharing their opinion

43. **keep one's cool**—to remain calm under pressure

44. **keep one's eyes peeled**—to keep close watch for

45. **keep one's fingers crossed**—to hope for good luck or for a desired result

46. **keep something to oneself**—to keep a secret

47. **keyed up**—nervous or excited

48. **knock oneself out**—to go out of one's way to do something, to work very hard

49. **(not to) know if one is coming or going**—to be undecided, in a state of confusion, often caused by overwork

50. **learn the ropes**—learn the details of performing an activity

51. **(a) load off one's mind**—good news that causes relief

52. **look on the bright side**—focus on the positive aspects

53. **lose one's temper**—to become very angry

54. **lose touch with**—to be out of contact

55. **lucky dog**—a person who is very fortunate

56. **make it**—to be successful

57. **make up**—to complete an activity at a time later than originally scheduled

58. **measure up**—to meet one's expectations

59. **miss the boat**—to let an opportunity slip away without taking advantage of it

60. **money to burn**—excess money

61. **monkey business**—comical or silly activities or dishonest acts

62. **name of the game**—the reason for doing something

63. **night owl**—a person who likes to stay out late at night

64. **not in your life**—never

65. **on sale**—marked down to a special price

66. **out on a limb**—in a position where one states his position openly at the risk of criticism or failure

67. **over one's head**—too difficult to understand

68. **play by ear**—to play music without written notes, or to perform in an unplanned, impromptu manner

69. **pooped out**—really tired

70. **pop the question**—ask a very important question, perhaps to propose marriage

71. **pull one's leg**—to joke with

72. **put the squeeze on**—to flirt with

73. **save for a rainy day**—to put away to enjoy in less profitable times (money)

74. **say a mouthful**—to say something of great importance or meaning

75. **see eye to eye**—to understand another person, to agree with

76. **(a) show of hands**—a way to count number of people who agree or disagree with something by raising hands

77. **skate on thin ice**—barely avoiding a big problem

78. **snake in the grass**—an evil, sneaky person

79. **something else**—really special

80. **something to crow about**—something outstanding that deserves to be bragged about

81. **stand one's ground**—to stay firm in one's belief or position

82. **steer clear of**—to avoid completely

83. **stick like glue**—to always be with someone

84. **stick one's neck out**—to express one's opinion even at the risk of being ridiculed

85. **straight from the horse's mouth**—said by someone directly involved

86. **strike it rich**—to be very lucky and acquire a large amount of money

87. **sweat out (the details)**—to work through the hard part

88. **(a) sure thing**—something that is certain not to change

89. **take a break**—have a rest from work

90. **take it easy**—to relax

91. **take up on something**—to accept an offer

92. **thumbs up (or down)**—to show approval (up) or disapproval (down)

93. **throw caution to the wind**—to act in a carefree manner, to do something dangerous or potentially harmful

94. **throw in the towel**—to give up on

95. **tide one over**—to last through a lean period (money or food)

96. **too big for one's britches**—with too much self assurance, an exaggerated feeling of self-worth

97. **tons**—a large quantity

98. **turn one's cheek**—to accept rejection or criticism without reacting negatively

99. **up in the air**—undecided, not confirmed

100. **wash one's hands of**—to forget about a problem or situation

APPENDIX E

50 COMMON USAGE ERRORS

The following list contains words that often cause usage errors. They are confusing because they sound alike or have similar meaning or spelling so it's easy to use the wrong word. This is a good list to review just before taking your TOEFL exam— you might be able to pick up a few extra points quickly by studying this carefully. Go over it completely a few times— once is probably not enough.

1. **A, AN**
    A is used before a word with a consonant sound, while AN is used before vowel sounds. Be careful with the letters *H, U,* and *O* (see the **CU**).

    A hurricane, but an honor. A university, but an uncle, A once-familiar face, but an orange.

2. **ACCEPT, EXCEPT**
    Please accept the award on my behalf.
    Everyone except Ernest is here.

3. **ACCESS, EXCESS**
    The young children were denied access to the R-rated movie.
    We were charged a fee by the airline for our excess baggage.

4. **ADVICE, ADVISE**
You should follow the <u>advice</u> of your parents.
Please <u>advise</u> me on how I might improve my TOEFL score.

5. **AFFECT, EFFECT**
The pollution <u>affects</u> everyone in the big city.
The <u>effect</u> of the herbal remedy is still being studied.

6. **AGAIN, AGAINST**
Please call me <u>again</u> next Monday.
The college teachers are demonstrating <u>against</u> their low salaries.

7. **ALLUSION, ILLUSION**
<u>ALLUSION</u> is an indirect reference, <u>ILLUSION</u> is something that appears real but isn't.

I accidentally made an <u>allusion</u> to his mother's death.
The <u>illusions</u> of magician David Copperfield are so outrageous as to be unbelievable.

8. **ALMOST, MOST**
<u>Almost</u> everyone well be present tonight.
<u>Most</u> people are afraid of snakes.

9. **ALREADY, ALL READY**
I have <u>already</u> called the fire department.
We're <u>all ready</u> to begin the trip.

10. **AMOUNT, NUMBER**
<u>AMOUNT</u> is used with non-countable nouns and <u>NUMBER</u> is used with count nouns.
The <u>number</u> of students, but the <u>amount</u> of time.

11. **BARELY, SCARCELY, HARDLY**
    These words all mean basically the same, but they are important because they are considered negative words. Avoid using them with other negative words.

    I can <u>barely</u> hear the teacher, NOT "I can <u>barely not</u>…"
    Also remember to use inverted word order if you begin a sentence with these words (see the **WO** section).

12. **BESIDE, BESIDES**
    The little girl sleeps with her doll <u>beside</u> her.
    <u>Besides</u> the TOEFL, I must also take the GMAT exam.

13. **BETWEEN, AMONG**
    <u>BETWEEN</u> is used only for two, and <u>AMONG</u> is used with three or more.

    <u>Between</u> you and me, I think that restaurant is too expensive.
    There is a great deal of interaction <u>among</u> the various departments of the hotel.

14. **CAPITAL, CAPITOL**
    Montgomery is the <u>capital</u> of Alabama. OR More <u>capital</u> will be required to finance the project.
    There will be no tours of the <u>capitol</u> today because Congress is in session.

15. **CLOTHES, CLOSE**
    I need to buy new <u>clothes</u>.
    Please <u>close</u> the door. OR The school is <u>close</u> to my home.

16. **COMPLEMENT, COMPLIMENT**
Both of these nouns can also be used as verbs.

This orange and blue tie will make a nice <u>complement</u> for my new blue suit.
Thanks very much for your kind <u>compliments</u>.

17. **CONSIDERABLE, CONSIDERATE**
The staff has gone to <u>considerable</u> lengths to make the new member feel welcomed.
It was very <u>considerate</u> of you to send the wedding gift.

18. **COSTUME, CUSTOM, CUSTOMS**
Mandy won the prize for best Halloween <u>costume</u>.
Most countries have distinct <u>customs</u>.
I hope I can get my new computer system through <u>customs</u> without paying too much in taxes.

19. **COUNCIL, COUSEL**
John is running for an office on the city <u>council.</u>
Ricky appreciated the <u>counsel</u> given to him by his student advisor.
His priest <u>counselled</u> him to go into drug rehabilitation.

20. **CREDIBLE, CREDITABLE**
Her version of the apparent crime was quite <u>credible</u>.
His <u>creditable</u> status had to be proved before he could secure financing for the car.

21. **DECENT, DESCENT**
A <u>decent</u> person would never take advantage of the elderly.
The pilot began his final <u>descent</u> into New York as he approached the La Guardia airport.

22. **DESERT, DESSERT**

It's good to remember a mental association to help avoid confusing these words. Here, notice the word dessert has two letter "s"s. Remember the ice-cream cone, a dessert, has a double scoop!

Many animals are adapted for living in the hot, dry <u>desert</u>.

For <u>dessert</u>, I'll have the hot fudge sundae with chocolate syrup and nuts.

23. **DEVICE, DEVISE**

The <u>device</u> uses only batteries.

Scientists struggled for years to <u>devise</u> a vaccine for the smallpox virus.

24. **DIFFER, DIFFERENT**

The new Volkswagen sedan <u>differs</u> enormously from the original.

It's refreshing to know people whose tastes are somewhat <u>different</u>.

25. **ELICIT, ILLICIT**

The letter to the editor <u>elicited</u> responses from numerous readers.

The use of <u>illicit</u> drugs is strictly prohibited on this campus.

26. **EXAMPLE, SAMPLE**

Grape juice changing to wine is an <u>example</u> of fermentation.

Publishing houses usually require <u>sample</u> work before offering book contracts.

27. **FARTHER, FURTHER**
FARTHER is only used with distance, FURTHER can be used for distance, but also for time, degree, and quantity.

Germany is much farther from China than Korea.
Further research is needed before conclusions can be drawn.

28. **FEWER, LESS**

FEWER is used only with count nouns, while LESS is used only with non-countable nouns.

FEWER coins, but LESS money, FEWER minutes, but LESS time.

29. **FORMER, FIRST**
FORMER refers to the first of two, while FIRST refers to the first of three or more.

Both halves of the basketball game were exciting, but the former seemed faster.
Carl was the first student from my class to be selected to receive a scholarship.

30. **FORMERLY, FORMALLY**
He formerly served on the board of directors.
Everyone at the embassy reception was dressed extremely formally.

31. **FORTH, FOURTH**
During the storm, the boat rocked back and forth.
Winning fourth place in the beauty contest was a disappointment for Brenda.

32. **HAD BETTER, WOULD RATHER**
You <u>had better</u> study for your TOEFL exam!
I <u>would rather</u> go to the beach for the weekend.

33. **IMAGINARY, IMAGINATIVE**
Alice in Wonderland is filled with <u>imaginary</u> characters.
Lewis Caroll's work was certainly <u>imaginative</u>.

34. **IMMORTAL, IMMORAL**
The music of Mozart in <u>immortal</u>.
The <u>immoral</u> behaviour of the child was a disappointment to her parents.

35. **INDUSTRIAL, INDUSTRIOUS**
The music major never planned on doing <u>industrial</u> word for a living.
Her success as a student is due to her <u>industrious</u> study habits.

36. **INSPIRE, ASPIRE**
The architect claims that his work was <u>inspired</u> by the music of Rachmaninoff.
She <u>aspires</u> to be a writer although her work has yet to be published.

37. **INTELLIGENT, INTELLIGIBLE**
Trading my car for a bicycle proved to be an <u>intelligent</u> decision.
Her accent is so strong that her English is hardly <u>intelligible</u>.

38. **ITS, IT'S**
The dog finally found <u>its</u> way home.
<u>It's</u> time to leave or we'll miss our flight for sure.

39. **KIND, SORT, TYPE**
These words have the same meaning, but remember they have plural forms that we often neglect to use.
One <u>KIND</u> but those <u>KINDS</u>. A <u>SORT</u>, but two <u>SORTS</u>.

40. **LATER, LATTER**
Would you like to go to the grocery store now or wait until <u>later</u>?
I like both restaurants, but the <u>latter</u> might be better if we plan to take the children.

41. **LIKE, AS IF, SUCH AS**
Bernard looks very much <u>like</u> his father.
The beans smell <u>as if</u> they are burning.
Woodwinds <u>such as</u> oboes, clarinets, and bassoons require the use of a reed.

42. **LONELY, ALONE**
Martha has felt <u>lonely</u> since her children have all left home.
Sometimes it's nice to be <u>alone</u>.

43. **LOOSE, LOOSEN, LOSE, LOSS**
The light bulb doesn't work because it's too <u>loose</u>.
Toward the end of the day the executives like to <u>loosen</u> their ties and roll up their sleeves.
Gambling is a good way to <u>lose</u> your money quickly.
The climb in interest rates caused the unexpected <u>loss</u> of money.

44. **MAYBE, MAY BE**
<u>Maybe</u> this rain will end soon and we can play football.
It <u>may be</u> time to have the car tuned up.

45. **PASSED, PAST**
I easily passed my exam this morning.
The boy ran past the house and continued around the block.
Sometimes it's better to think of the future instead of dwelling on the past.

46. **PERSONAL, PERSONNEL**
Whom I voted for is personal.
We have a personnel meeting this afternoon.

47. **QUIET, QUITE, QUIT**
You must remain quiet in the library.
It's quite cold today.
Julian decided to quit his job after 15 years.

48. **THOROUGH, THROUGH**
A thorough physical exam is a good idea if you plan to start training for the marathon.
My cat loves to spend hours looking through the window.

49. **WEATHER, WHETHER**
We're expecting beautiful weather for the concert.
I haven't decided whether to buy a car now or wait for the new models.

50. **WHO'S, WHOSE**
Who's your English teacher this semester?
Does anyone know whose book this is?

APPENDIX F

VERB TENSE MODELS

SIMPLE PRESENT TENSE
Remember to add an "s" in the third person singular.

I walk
You walk
He, she, it walks
We, you, they walk

PERSENT PERFECT TENSE
Remember to use "has" in the third person singular.

I have walked
You have walked
He, she, it has walked
We, you, they have walked

PRESENT CONTINOUS TENSE
Here, we conjugate the verb *to be* like the simple present tense.

I am walking
You are walking
He, she, it is walking
We, you, they are walking

PRESENT PERFECT CONTINOUS TENSE

Here, we conjugate the verb *to have* in the simple present tense
and use "been".

I have been walking
You have been walking
He, she, it has been walking
We, you, they have been walking

SIMPLE PAST TENSE

Here, we simply add "ed" to all conjugations, unless the verb
is irregular, in which case we use the irregular form for all
conjugations.

I walked
You walked
He, she, it walked
We, you, they walked

PAST PERFECT TENSE

Here, we use *had* with a past participle.

I had walked
You had waked
He, she, it had walked
We, you, they had walked

PAST CONTINOUS TENSE

Here, we conjugate the verb *to be* in the past tense.

I was walking
You were walking
He, she, it was walking
We, you, they were walking

PAST PERFECT CONTINOUS TENSE

Here, we use *had been* in each conjugation.

I had been walking
You had been walking
He, she, it had been walking
We, you, they had been walking

SIMPLE FUTURE TENSE (WITH WILL)

Here, we use the word *will* with the simple form of a verb.

I will walk
You will walk
He, she, it will walk
We, you, they will walk

FUTIRE WITH "GOING TO" TENSE

Here, we use a conjugated form of the verb *to be*, the words
going to, and the simple form of a verb.

I am going to walk
You are going to walk
He, she, it is going to walk
We, you, they are going to walk

FUTURE PERFECT TENSE

Here, we use *will, have,* and a past participle.

I will have walked
You will have walked
He, she, it will have walked
We, you, they will have walked

FUTURE CONTINOUS TENSE

Here, we use *will be* with a present participle.

I will be walking
You will be walking
He, she, it will be walking
We, you, they will be walking

FUTURE PERFECT CONTINOUS TENSE

Here, we use *will, have, been,* and a present participle.

I will have been walking
You will have been walking
He, she, it will have been walking
We, you, they will have been walking

APPENDIX G

PREPOSITION COMBINATIONS

Review these well, as they cause problems for many Hindi speakers. They don't follow rules—they must be learned by example.

A *absent from, accustomed to, add to, acquainted with, admire for, afraid of, agree with/on/about something, angry at/with, apologize to, apply to, approve of, agree with, arrange to, arrive at/in, ask about/for, aware of*

B *bad for, believe in, belong to, bored with/by, borrow from*

C *capable of, clear to, command to, compare to/with, complain to/about, composed of, concentrate on, conscious of, consists of, crazy about, crowded with*

D *depend on/upon, decide to, devoted to, determined by, delighted by, differ in, disagree with, disappointed in, discuss with, divide into, divorced from, done with, dream about/of*

E *enable to, encouraged by, engaged to, equal to, escape from, excited about/by, excuse for, excused from, exhausted from*

F *familiar with, forgive for, friendly to/with, frightened of/by, fulfilled by, full of*

G *get rid of, giggle at, gone from, good for, graduate from*

H *happen to, hear about/of, hear from, help with, hide from, hope for, humbled by, humiliated by, hungry for*

I *impressed by, informed of, insist in, instruct to, interested in, intrigued by, introduce to, invite to, involved in*

J *joke at/with, jot down, judge by/from, jump at, justified by*

K *kind to, know about/of, known as*

L *laugh at, listen to, loan to, look at, look for/forward to*

M *mad at, made of, married to, matter to*

P *participate in, pay for, patient with, pleased with, point at/out, polite to, prepared for/to, protect from, proud of*

S *satisfied with, scared of/by, search for, separate from, similar to, sorry about/for, speak to/with, specialized in, stare at, subtract from, sure of, surprised by*

T *take care of, talk to/with/about, tell about/to, terrified of/by thankful for, thirsty for, threatened by, tolerant of, tired of/from, train in, travel to*

W *wait for/on, wish for, worried about*

APPENDIX H

SCORE CALCULATION TABLE

Note: Even though this edition does not include practice exams they are widely available and you should take a few before you take the actual TOEFL. This table will give you an approximate score, based on the number of correct answers in each section. See the following appendix to convert this score to the iBT scale.

To get an overall score, take your three converted scores (one from each section), add them together, divide by three, then multiply by ten.

N° CORECT	SECTION 1	SECTION 2	SECTION 3
50	68	-	68
49	66	-	66
48	64	-	64
47	63	-	63
46	62	-	62
45	61	-	61
44	60	-	61
43	59	-	59
42	58	-	58
41	57	-	58
40	57	68	57
39	56	65	56
38	55	64	55
37	54	63	55
36	53	61	54
35	53	59	53

34	52	58	52
33	51	57	51
32	51	56	51
31	50	54	50
30	49	53	49
29	49	52	49
28	48	51	48
27	48	50	48
26	47	49	47
25	47	48	47
24	46	47	46
23	45	46	45
22	45	45	45
21	44	44	44
20	43	43	43
19	43	42	43
18	42	41	42
17	42	40	42
16	41	39	41
15	40	38	40
14	39	37	39
13	38	36	38
12	37	35	37
11	36	34	36
10	35	34	35
9	33	33	33
8	32	31	32
7	31	30	31
6	30	28	30
5	29	26	29
4	28	25	28
3-2-1-0	27-25-22-20	24-23-21-20	27-25-22-20

APPENDIX I

TOTAL SCORE COMPARISION CHART

ITP..................iBT

677..............120
650..............115
640..............112
630..............109
620..............105
610..............102
600..............100
590..............96
580..............92
570..............88
560..............83
550..............83
540..............76
530..............71
520..............68
510..............64
500..............60
490..............57
480..............54
470..............52
460..............48
450..............45
440..............42
430..............39
420..............36
400..............32

ANSWER KEY

SWE-2:	2. 3, Fishing 3. 2, This 4. 3, Breathing 5. 5, Whoever finds the lost puppy 6. 1, Tornadoes 7. 4, To drive 8. 1, Mumps 9. 1, Papyrus 10. 3, Falling 11. 5, That pigeons can find their way home 12. 1, Subjects 13. 4, To study 14. 1, Silk 15. 3, Advertising
SWE-3:	2. will begin blooming 3. should have been, was reached 4. is 5. are 6. is spoken 7. was sued 8. was, is considered 9. is done 10. will be 11. has seen 12. has given 13. are discouraged 14. is considered to be 15. are, score
MINI TOEFL-1	1. C, 2. B, 3. A, 4. B, 5. C, 6. A, 7. D, 8. A, 9. B, 10. B
SWE-4	2. B, 3. NV, 4. B, 5. B, 6. B, 7. AV, 8. B, 9. NV, 10. B, 11. B, 12. B, 13. B, 14. B, 15. B, 16. B, 17. B, 18. B, 19. AV, 20. B
SWE-5	2. V, 3. V, 4. X, 5. V, 6. X, 7. V, 8. X, 9. X, 10. X, 11. V, 12. X, 13. X, 14. V, 15. V, 16. V, 17. V, 18. X, 19. X, 20. V
SWE-6	2. P, 3. P, 4. C, 5. C, 6. C, 7. C, 8. C, 9. P, 10. P, 11. C, 12. P, 13. P, 14. C, 15. C
SWE-7	2. – 3. ✔ 4. + 5. – 6. ✔ 7. – 8. – 9. + 10. ✔ 11. ✔ 12. – 13. + 14. – 15. –
MINI TOEFL-2	1. B, 2. C, 3. D, 4. A, 5. B, 6. A, 7. B, 8. A, 9. B, 10. C

SWE-9 2. MC, 3. SC, 4. MC, 5. SC, 6. MC, 7. SC, 8. SC, 9. SC, 10. MC, 11. MC, 12. SC, 13. SC, 14. SC, 15. SC

SWE-10 2. X, 3. SC, 4. SC, 5. X, 6. SC, 7. SC, 8. X, 9. X, 10. SC, 11. SC, 12. X, 13. SC, 14. SC, 15. SC

SWE-11 2. X, 3. X, 4. SC, 5. X, 6. MC, 7. X, 8. X, 9. MC, 10. SC, 11. X, 12. SC, 13. X, 14. X, 15. SC

MINI TOEFL-3 1. C, 2. A, 3. B, 4. D, 5. C, 6. A, 7. C, 8. B, 9. A, 10. C

SWE-12 2. X, 3. NC, that we won the game 4. NC, how children acquire a second language 5. NC, Where we shop for fresh vegetables 6. NC, that the Tooth Fairy really exists 7. NC, That it infrequently rains in the desert 8. X, 9. X, 10. NC, How much money the politician spent on his campaign 11. NC, That cigarettes cause cancer 12. NC, that about 95% of the population is right handed 13. NC, that no two fingerprints are the same 14. NC, how to operate the microwave oven 15. NC, How twins interact during childhood 16. NC, that the game had to be cancelled because of bad weather 17. NC, that his project is the best 18. NC, that dogs and cats are color blind 19. NC, How the brain functions 20. X

SWE-13
2. he wanted to be a fireman 3. the man had run a red light 4. the congressman will lose the election 5. the patient was in stable condition 6. crystals have healing powers 7. the new law had been passed 8. we will score above 500 on the TOEFL 9. we will have a fire drill today 10. carbohydrates be limited

SWE-14
2. which the skunk discharges 3. which are located near the base of the skunk's tail 4. which can be smelled from half a mile away 5. which can also sting the eyes 6. skunks eat 7. scientists have classified 8. skunks typically reach 9. the skunk must avoid 10. scientists have found in South America

MINI TOEFL-4
1. D, 2. B, 3. B, 4. C, 5. A, 6. B, 7. B, 8. C, 9. A, 10. D

SWE-15
2. (Garcia...name), Chang...world 3. (Christmas...December 25), Even though...Jesus Christ 4. (the secret...men), since...1886 5. (it...fly), Because...bird, although...hour 6. (he...school), Unless...bicycle, even though...time 7. (the flower...Asia), Although...tulips 8. Until...invented, (writers...typewriters), even though...tedious 9. (The university...week), so that...taken, before...begins 10.(Tickets...expensive), although...available, if...minute 11.(Please...staff), as soon as...know, if...planned 12. (we...game), Unless...Saturday 13. (you...discounts), if...early, although...penalized 14. (Tony...sleeping), When...rang, although...wake up 15. (The light...rainbow), although...sun

SWE-16   2. SC, ADV 3. MC 4. SC, ADV 5. SC, ADJ 6. MC 7. SC, ADV 8. MC 9. SC, ADJ 10. X 11. SC, ADJ 12. SC, N 13. SC, ADV 14. SC, N 15. MC

SWE-17   2. 3, 3. 1, 4. 3, 5. 4, 6. 1, 7. 2, 8. 4, 9. 1, 10. 3, 11. 3, 12. 2, 13. 2, 14. 4, 15. 2

MINI TOEFL-5   1. A, 2. D, 3. B, 4. B, 5. C, 6. D, 7. A, 8. A, 9. C, 10. A

SWE-19   2. team, are 3. Japanese, are 4. data, are 5. Deer, are 6. All, are 7. candles, are 8. pilots, are 9. Alumni, are 10. Ana, is 11. English, is 12. results, are 13. Some, are 14. police, is 15. All, are

MINI TOEFL-6   1. A, 2. D, 3. C, 4. A, 5. C, 6. C, 7. B, 8. A, 9. C, 10. A

SWE-20   2. is 3. are 4. is 5. are 6. is 7. are 8. is 9. are 10. are 11. is 12. are 13. is 14. is 15. is

SWE-21   2. history, is 3. cholera, is 4. *Essential Spanish for Tourists*, provides 5. Everyone, has 6. secretaries, have 7. players, referees, are 8. check, was 9. van, is 10. Some, has 11. attendant, usher (preceded by every), is 12. crimes (preceded by the number of), has 13. pair, is 14. school, was 15. It, was

MINI TOEFL-7   1. D , 2. A, 3. B, 4. C, 5. C, 6. A, 7. A, 8. B, 9. B, 10. B

SWE-23   2. their 3. her 4. his 5. our 6. his 7. his 8. their 9. our 10. his

SWE-24   2. its 3. their 4. its 5. their 6. its 7. their 8. their 9. its 10. her

SWE-25   2. Everyone has to present his... 3. ...is going to order its new... 4. The one million dollars was given...who won it... 5. ...are popular... because of their warm... 6. ... is available... students request it. 7. ...his pet...for his actions. 8. Everyone needs to take his... 9. Many a man has... 10. books have...they would disappear.

MINI TOEFL-8   1. D, 2. C, 3. A, 4. D, 5. B, 6. C, 7. D, 8. A, 9. C, 10. C

SWE-27   2. X, for some time now, (is planning) 3. X, since the end of the football season, (is) 4. ✓, So far, (have been reached) 5. ✓, up until now, (has been found) 6. X, When she died, (has...been) 7. X, By the end of the class, (will had finished) 8. X, In the early seventies, (is recording) 9. ✓, since this morning, (has been dropping) 10. X, By the time we get home, (will had arrive)

SWE-28   2. hold/held 3. wrote/written 4. lived/live 5. became/become 6. discovering/discovered 7. wrote/written 8. made/make 9. have gave/have given 10. give/given 11. make/made 12. know/known 13. bit/bitten 14. sworn/swore 15. became/become

MINI TOEFL-9 1. A, 2. A, 3. D, 4. B, 5. A, 6. C, 7. B, 8. A, 9. C, 10. A

SWE-30: (top to bottom; line by line) my, yourself, his, her, its, our, yours, them, oneself, who

SWE-31: 2. O 3. PA 4. PP 5. R 6. S 7. PA 8. PP 9. PA 10. O 11. S 12. PA 13. PA 14. R 15. S

MINI TOEFL-10 1. A, 2. C, 3. D, 4. A, 5. D, 6. A, 7. A, 8. C, 9. A, 10. B

SWE-32: 2. X 3. ✓ 4. ✓ 5. X 6. X 7. ✓ 8. ✓ 9. ✓ 10. X

SWE-33: 2. X 3. ✓ 4. ✓ 5. X 6. X 7. ✓ 8. ✓ 9. ✓ 10. X

SWE-34: 2. ✓ 3. ✓ 4. X 5. X 6. ✓ 7. ✓ 8. X 9. ✓ 10. ✓

SWE-35: 2. ✓ 3. X 4. ✓ 5. X 6. ✓ 7. X 8. ✓ 9. ✓ 10. ✓

SWE-36: 2. X 3. ✓ 4. ✓ 5. ✓ 6. ✓ 7. ✓ 8. X 9. ✓ 10. X

MINI TOEFL-11 1. A, 2. C, 3. D, 4. A, 5. D, 6. A, 7. A, 8. C, 9. A, 10. B

SWE-37: 2. ✓ 3. X 4. ✓ 5. ✓ 6. ✓ 7. ✓ 8. X 9. ✓ 10. X 11. ✓ 12. ✓ 13. ✓ 14. ✓ 15. X

SWE-39: 2. PREP 3. INF 4. INF 5. INF 6. PREP 7. INF 8. INF 9. PREP 10. INF 11. INF 12. INF 13. INF 14. INF 15. INF 16. PREP 17. INF 18. PREP 19. PREP 20. PREP

SWE-40: 2. S-We, V-go, I-to learn 3. IS-To drive, V-is 4. S-Jesus, V-wants, I-to drive 5. S-Doctors, V-need, I-to keep 6. S-She, V-went, I-to buy 7. IS-To control, V-spray 8. S-Researchers, V-hope, I-to find 9. IS-To eat, V-is 10. S-I, V-want, I-to see 11. S-band, V-is going, I-to perform 12. S-Giovanna, V-likes, I-to cook 13. S-We, V-plan, I-to put 14. S-We, V-need, I-to plan 15. S-I, V-hope, I-to make

SWE-41: 2. S-grandmother, V-is arriving 3. S-They, V-enjoy, G-playing 4. GS-Backpacking, V-requires 5. S-orchestra, V-is practicing 6. GS-Learning, V-is 7. S-He, V-is becoming, G-playing 8. GS-Flooding, V-was caused, G-breaking 9. GS-Mailing, V-insures 10. S-players, V-are becoming 11. S-She, V-thanked, G-babysitting 12. GS-Swimming, V-is 13. S-family, V-is going 14. GS-Roller-blading, V-is 15. S-Greg Louganis, V-perfected, G-diving

MINI TOEFL-12 1. C, 2. B, 3. D, 4. A, 5. D, 6. A, 7. B, 8. C, 9. C, 10. A

SWE-42: 2. (grown), (hanging) 3. (recruited), (scheduled) 4. (bubbling) 5. (showing), (aspiring) 6. (playing) 7. (Folding), (exhausted) 8. (swimming) 9. (accused), (coming) 10. (selling), (barking) 11. (torn), (experienced) 12. (Neglected), (abused) 13. (circulating), (polluted) 14. (reserved) 15. (tossed), (shredded), (sliced), (grated)

SWE-43:   Active Verbs: is walking, are playing, were helping, looks, was put, will call, have been fed, drank, are studying, is cooking; Verbal Adjectives: selling, speaking, eating, acting, participating, looking, remembering, reviewing, jumping, crying

SWE-44:   2. convincing, convinced 3. surprising, surprised 4. annoying, annoyed 5. exhausting, exhausted 6. entertaining, entertained 7. frightening, frightened 8. amusing, amused 9. entertaining, entertained 10. exciting, excited

SWE-45:   2. A, 3. B, 4. A, 5. B, 6. B, 7. A, 8. A, 9. B, 10. B

SWE-46:   2. X, 3. OK, 4. X, 5. OK, 6. X, 7. OK, 8. X, 9. OK, 10. OK

SWE-47:   2. Winning the election...or Having won the election... 3. After running all the way home... 4. Having a high caffeine content... 5. After graduating from college... 6. Requiring little water... 7. Being easy to grow... 8. After being checked... 9. When consumed frequently... 10. Being high in calories...

SWE-48: 2. applying, TOEFL exam, X 3. cleaning, maid, OK 4. eating, stomachache, X 5. Standing, sun, X 6. Made, pie, OK 7. Arriving, Christina, OK 8. Running, blood pressure, X 9. Living, couple, OK 10. Loving, performance, X 11. Considering, parties, X 12. Considered, works, X 13. Offering, store, OK 14. Located, Texas, OK 15. Powered, electric cars, OK 16. Practicing, routine, X 17. being carried, arrangement, OK 18. working, Manuel's eyes, X 19. plugging, electrical shock, X 20. Having spent, shopper, OK

MINI TOEFL-13 1. B, 2. D, 3. A, 4. B, 5. B, 6. B, 7. C, 8. A, 9. A, 10. A

SWE-50: 2. delivery 3. trial 4. withdrawal 5. acceptance 6. movement 7. examination 8. discovery 9. pleasure 10. erasure 11. refusal 12. advertisement 13. observation 14. judgement 15. existence 16. pressure 17. recovery 18. correspondence 19. formation 20. obligation

SWE-51: 2. Flattery, flatter 3. existence, exist 4. mastery, master, 5. advertisement, advertise 6. decorations, decorate 7. conclusions, conclude 8. refusal, refuse 9. correspondence, correspond 10. executions, execute 11. coherence, cohere 12. pleasures, please 13. concealment, conceal 14. examination, examine 15. encouragement, encourage

SWE-52:

2. decision 3. preference 4. resignation 5. refusal 6. OK 7. recovery 8. abandonment 9. installation 10. erasure 11. excitement 12. OK 13. existence 14. implication 15. transfer 16. division 17. pressure 18. automation 19. departure 20. arrangement

SWE-53:

2. OK 3. resigning, resignation 4. OK 5. failing, failure 6. arranging, arrangement 7. developing, development 8. informing, information 9. OK 10. implying, implication 11. withdrawings, withdrawals 12. agreeing, agreement 13. discovering, discovery 14. existing, existence 15. OK

MINI TOEFL-14: 1. D, 2. B, 3. A, 4. B, 5. C, 6. B, 7. B, 8. C, 9. A, 10. B

SWE-54:

2. alcoholic 3. inventor 4. socialite 5. magician 6. youngster 7. servant 8. carpenter 9. racketeer 10. biologist

SWE-55:

2. penniless 3. golden 4. Nebraskan 5. introductory 6. selfish 7. fireproof 8. majestic 9. impressionable 10. picturesque 11. fanatical 12. ghostly 13. awesome 14. active 15. glamorous 16. chilly

SWE-56:

2. ADJ 3. ADJ 4. ADV 5. ADV 6. ADV 7. ADV 8. ADJ 9. ADV 10. ADV 11. ADV 12. ADV 13. ADJ 14. ADV 15. ADJ 16. ADJ 17. ADV 18. ADV 19. ADJ 20. ADV

SWE-57: 1. excel, excellent, excellently 2. satisfaction, satisfy, satisfactorily 3. confidence, confide, confidential 4. success, successful, successfully 5. decide, decisive, decisively 6. energy, energize, energetically 7. excess, exceed, excessive 8. repetition, repetitive, repetitively 9. categorize, categorical, categorically 10. imagination, imagine, imaginatively

MINI TOEFL-15: 1. B, 2. D, 3. A, 4. C, 5. A, 6. D, 7. A, 8. A, 9. A, 10. B

SWE-58: 2. quiet 3. angrily 4. wonderful 5. carefully 6. quiet 7. pale 8. sad 9. good 10. crazy 11. carefully 12. wide 13. honest 14. brightly 15. angry 16. finally 17. good 18. uncontrollably 19. sweet 20. happy

SWE-59: 2. highly 3. extremely 4. extreme 5. highly 6. really 7. real 8. extremely 9. original 10. extreme

SWE-60: 1. happier, happiest 2. more/most 3. wiser, wisest 4. more/most 5. messier, messiest 6. better, best 7. longer, longest 8. funnier, funniest 9. more/most 10. greener, greenest 11. worse, worst 12. more/most 13. faster, fastest 14. more/most 15. more/most 16. stranger, strangest 17. more/most 18 more/most 19. lazier, laziest 20. crazier, craziest

SWE-61: 2. more 3. better 4. better 5. tallest 6. more 7. less 8. faster 9. easiest 10. with 11. more exhausted 12. best 13. tallest 14. best 15. less

MINI TOEFL-16: 1. D, 2. A, 3. B, 4. C, 5. D, 6. B, 7. B, 8. B, 9. B, 10. B

SWE-63: 2. Only once has Damon forgotten... 3. Scarcely had I sat down... 4. Only after he passed the TOEFL did he begin... 5. Only once have I gone... 6. Never before have I seen... 7. Nowhere is the price... 8. Not only did we go... 9. Only in the morning does the doctor see... 10. Rarely does it snow... 11. Only after doing extensive research did the doctoral candidate begin... 12. At no time were the concert goers allowed... 13. Nowhere have I enjoyed... 14. Only after practicing for hours could she play... 15. Only on Sunday are the museums...

SWE-64: 2. So hungry were the children... 3. There are many important reasons 4. Here are the answers... 5. Little does the boy know... 6. In walked the judge... 7. Such a desire to win is not healthy... 8. Few literary works include such... 9. Up rose the smoke... 10. Out ran the children... 11. So clever was the thief... 12. Such animals are common... 13. Here are the books... 14. So talented was she... 15. Few were the nights...

MINI TOEFL-17: 1. A, 2. C, 3. D, 4. A, 5. C, 6. A, 7. D, 8. A, 9. A, 10. B

SWE-65: 2. Under the table are... 3. Seen at the awards presentation were... OR At the awards presentation were seen... 4. Somewhere over the rainbow is... 5. Discovered in the basket was... OR In the basket was discovered... 6. Should he go... 7. Around the corner lives... 8. Engaged to be married was... 9. Had he read... 10. At the top of the mountain waited... 11. Accused of the crime were... 12. Stored in the big trunk are... 13. In the trunk of the car is... 14. Should you see it... 15. Placed at the top of the Christmas tree was...

SWE-66: 2. D? 3. I? 4. D? 5. I? 6. I? 7. I? 8. I? 9. I? 10. D? 11. I? 12. I? 13. I? 14. D? 15. I? 16. D? 17. I? 18. D? 19. I? 20. I?

SWE-67: 2. ...we will have tomorrow? 3. ...when we will return... 4. ...how much money I can borrow. 5. ...why the alarm was sounded. 6. ...how the movie ended. 7. ...how much postage the letter needs. 8. ...where the event took place. 9. ...how much the book costs. 10. ...what the final score will be.

MINI TOEFL-18 1. C, 2. D, 3. A, 4. C, 5. A, 6. B, 7. B, 8. B, 9. A, 10. C

SWE-69: 2. a glass of wine 3. eating 4. because of her hard work 5. agreement 6. washing the dishes 7. medicine 8. six 9. in 10. because it was comfortable 11. frequently 12. to do 13. enjoyable 14. to tackle 15. misbehave

SWE-70: 2. X, 3. OK, 4. X, 5. OK, 6. OK, 7. X, 8. X 9. X 10. X

SWE-71: 2. X, 3. OK, 4. OK, 5. X, 6. X, 7. X, 8. X, 9. X, 10 X, 11. OK, 12. X, 13. OK, 14. OK, 15. OK

SWE-72: 2. ...much redder than those on that tree. 3. ...than yours. 4. You should pick up not only... 5. ...than any other state... 6. ...and where we will stay. 7. ...just as exciting as... 8. ...greater than that of... 9. ...and eating chocolate... 10. ...because of many mistakes. 11. ...played tennis. 12. ...as expensive as... 13. ...or to your department head. 14. The band marched... 15. ... than any other city...

MINI TOEFL-19: 1. C, 2. A, 3. D, 4. B, 5. D, 6. D, 7. C, 8. A, 9. D, 10. A

SWE-74: (Sample answers—many more could be used) 2. right, accurate 3. beautiful, cute 4. big, huge 5. complete, whole 6. start, begin 7. quick, rapid 8. multi-colored, vivid 9. elegant, sophisticated 10. jump, spring 11. humid, damp 12. auto, vehicle 13. advertising, commercials 14. stare, watch 15. rarely, hardly ever

SWE-75: 2. ↑ 3. = 4. ↓ 5. ↑ 6. ↑ 7. = 8. ↓ 9. ↓ 10. ↓ 11. = 12. ↓   13. ↑ 14. ↓ 15. ↑

SWE-76: 2. X, 3. OK, 4. X 5. X, 6. OK, 7. X, 8. X, 9. X, 10. X, 11. OK, 12 X, 13. X, 14. OK, 15. X

MINI TOEFL-20: 1. C, 2. B, 3. A, 4. A, 5. D, 6. C, 7. C, 8. C, 9. A, 10. D

SWE-78: 2. an, 3. a, 4. a, 5. a, 6. a, 7. a, 8. a, 9. a, 10. an, 11. a, 12. an, 13. an, 14. an, 15. an, 16. a, 17. a, 18. an, 19. a, 20. a

SWE-79:   2. a Cherokee, the 3. in the, a, of the 4. The, the, the 5. the, the west, of the 6. the hope, a 7. of, the, a 8. is the, of the 9. Chinese, the 10. the most, the, the

MINI TOEFL-21: 1. D, 2. A, 3. C, 4. C, 5. A, 6. A, 7. A, 8. B, 9. D, 10. D

SWE-80:   MAKE: appointment, arrangements, tone, comparison, effort, friends, turn, plans, speech, discovery, proposal, money, recommendation DO: dishes, bed, best, homework, laundry, research, housework, business

SWE-81:   2. laid 3. lie 4. rises 5. lay 6. rise 7. raise 8. rise 9. raised 10. raise 11. laid 12. set 13. sitting 14. lying 15. raise

SWE-82:   2. 2, 3. 2, 4. 2, 5. 2, 6. 3+, 7. 2, 8. 3+, 9. 3+, 10. 2, 11. 2, 12. 2, 13. 3+, 14. 2, 15. 2, 16. 2, 17. 3+, 18. 2, 19. 3+, 20. 3+

SWE-83:   2. B, 3. A, 4. B, 5. A, 6. B, 7. B, 8. A, 9. B, 10. A

SWE-84:   2. NC 3. NC 4. C 5. NC 6. NC 7. C 8. C 9. NC 10. NC 11. C 12. C 13. NC 14. NC 15. C 16. C 17. NC 18. NC 19. C 20. C

SWE-85:   2. C 3. NC 4. B 5. C 6. C 7. C 8. NC 9. C 10. NC 11. C 12. B 13. C 14. NC 15. B

SWE-86:   2. A, 3. A, 4. A, 5. B, 6. A, 7. B, 8. A, 9. A, 10. A

SWE-87:   2. X, 3. OK, 4. OK, 5. OK, 6. X, 7. X, 8. X, 9. X, 10. OK, 11. X, 12. X, 13. X, 14. X, 15. OK

MINI TOEFL-22: 1. D, 2. B, 3. B, 4. A, 5. D, 6. A, 7. C, 8. A, 9. A, 10. A

L-2: 1. B, 2. A, 3. B, 4. B, 5. B, 6. A, 7. B, 8. B, 9. B, 10. B, 11. A, 12. B, 13. A, 14. B, 15. B

L-3: 1. B, 2. B, 3. B, 4. A, 5. B, 6. B, 7. A, 8. A, 9. A, 10. A, 11. B, 12. A, 13. B, 14. B, 15. B

ABOUT THE AUTHOR: Greg Britt is the Director of Britt Servicios Lingüísticos, an institute in Mexico City that specializes in TOEFL preparation (see www.dfbritt.com). He previously taught English at the Monterrey Institute of Technology and Advanced Studies in Mexico City. Britt has also written a restaurant review column that has been published in *The Mexico City Times*, *The Herald* (international edition of the *Miami Herald*), and *The News*.

Titles by Greg Britt include:

TOEFL Prep for Spanish Speakers
TOEFL Prep for Chinese Speakers
(Video courses available for both, see www.etoeflprep.com)

5-Step TOEFL Prep for Advanced Students
5-Step TOEFL Prep for Arabic Speakers
5-Step TOEFL Prep for Chinese Speakers
5-Step TOEFL Prep for French Speakers
5-Step TOEFL Prep for German Speakers
5-Step TOEFL Prep for Greek Speakers
5-Step TOEFL Prep for Hindi Speakers
5-Step TOEFL Prep for Japanese Speakers
5-Step TOEFL Prep for Korean Speakers
5-Step TOEFL Prep for Portuguese Speakers
5-Step TOEFL Prep for Russian Speakers
5-Step TOEFL Prep for Spanish Speakers
(Info. at **www.5steptoeflprep.com**)

Advanced Grammar & TOEFL Prep with Marathi Notes